The Artisan teacher

A Field Guide to Skillful Teaching

MIKE RUTHERFORD

RUTHERFORD LEARNING GROUP
Professional Development for Educators

MW01003135

The Artisan Teacher: A Field Guide to Skillful Teaching

Published by Rutherford Learning Group, Inc.
6068 Oxfordshire Rd.
Weddington, NC 28173

© 2013 by Mike Rutherford, Ed.D.
All rights reserved.
Printed and bound in the United States of America

All rights reserved by the author. No part of this book may be used or reproduced in any manner whatsoever without written permission except in the case of brief quotations used in articles and reviews. The author is responsible for all content.

Cover and interior book design by Larry W. Van Hoose
Illustrations by Laurette Clark Wolfe

ISBN No. 978-0-9914724-0-6

Dedication

I dedicate this field guide to the memory of my father, Claude H. Rutherford, whose life illustrated the transformational power of education and diligence.

He was my first and best teacher.

Table of Contents

Table of Contents (continued)

Foreword 

I have an incurable curiosity for teaching. For over three decades, I've been teaching, observing teachers, and studying teaching. In that time, I've personally observed at least ten thousand episodes of classroom instruction and have spoken with colleagues about thousands more. Since it is generally fulfilling to satisfy one's curiosities, it has been a labor of love and not a bit of drudgery. Contrary to what one might imagine, these thousands of observations have never seemed repetitive or redundant. There is always something new to see, and, the more I look, the more I'm convinced that there are hundreds of ways to be excellent as a teacher.

Early on, I was expecting to be able to quickly spot some consistent actions that would support a template for describing successful teaching. I wished to say that all successful teachers do the same few things. Then I could logically tell other teachers, "Do these few things and you'll be successful too." As it turns out, successful teachers are successful in many ways. Some are well organized, but others, equally successful, are more spontaneous. Many effective teachers are energetic and enthusiastic, yet some excellent performers are quite low key. Some teachers are straightforward and businesslike and produce good results. Still others produce good results through a friendly, relaxed classroom climate. This is not to say that there are not observable, recurring patterns of instruction that especially successful teachers employ. There certainly are, and the remaining pages of this field guide are devoted to describing them. But there are many of them, and teachers employ them in many combinations and in many degrees. Successful teaching is a complex act.

A consistent, recurring pattern has emerged through all these observations. The most successful teachers are skillful. They *do* things. They make *moves*. They teach with an attention to detail and a level of execution that produces extra success for learners. They see teaching as a set of skills, some natural and some learned, that combine to produce optimal learning for students. As I have thought about this skillful approach and how it might be best described, I am reminded of an old term that has recently enjoyed a renaissance. The term is *Artisan*. The teachers who best exemplify this skillful approach to instruction are *Artisan Teachers*; skilled in the craft of teaching.

The word artisan, when used as an adjective, connotes a high quality, hand-made, unique nature. An artisan "this or that" implies that a craftsperson created a product in small batches, applying specialized knowledge and skill, with a measure of artistic creativity. We often hear of artisan bread, artisan cheese, or artisan jewelry. Historically, the word artisan is a noun. An artisan is a craftsperson. An artisan makes things. Stonemasons, coppersmiths, bakers, tanners, playwrights, songwriters, and tailors are artisans. The fruits of their labor have utility. They create items of value. The item's value is not entirely based on utility, however. It is also based on beauty, design, and delight. An artisan creates an item that is not only sturdy and functional, but beautiful and delightful to use.

Artisans are not purely artists, though artistic expression is found in their work. Artisans are not purely scientists, though scientific knowledge is essential to their work. Artisans are not merely technicians, though skilled labor is the core expression of their work. An artisan is one skilled in the applied arts, a craftsperson... a unique combination of artist, scientist, and skilled laborer. Excellent teachers are just like this. They are Artisans-artful, knowledgeable, skilled, masters of their craft (Rutherford, 2009a, p. 1).

An important hallmark of a profession, as opposed to an occupation, is that professionals practice based on an established body of knowledge for the benefit of clients. Physicians practice according to an established medical body of knowledge for the benefit of patients. Attorneys practice according to an established body of legal knowledge on behalf of clients. Airline pilots practice according to an established body of aviation knowledge on behalf of passengers. And educators, if we claim to be professionals too, should practice according to an established body of educational knowledge on behalf of our students. Further evidence of this professional approach is found in the use of a common lexicon of terms that describe and illustrate patterns of professional knowledge and practice. Medical Doctors speak and collaborate using terms from a common, scientific lexicon known and spoken by all physicians. Attorneys and airline pilots do the same thing. When this common, scientific lexicon is used, collaboration is clearer, faster, and less prone to error.

I was visiting a friend in the hospital one evening and stepped onto an elevator with two physicians who were talking about a patient. As they spoke, I felt a bit uneasy since I knew I should not be privy to the patient's medical condition. Then I realized that I had yet to understand a single word they said. The patient's privacy was safe. Why? The physicians were using their shared scientific language, a language I didn't understand. I also noticed that, even though the elevator trip was short, the physicians seemed to accomplish a good deal of collaboration. These are the fruits of a common lexicon; speed of communication, clarity of meaning, and fewer errors due to misconception or misunderstanding.

A common lexicon enhances educators' abilities to see patterns of effectiveness rather than only individual instances of effectiveness (Bransford, Brown, & Cocking, 2000). Pattern recognition is enhanced when the patterns have commonly understood names and characteristics. In a study where expert and novice physics teachers were shown video of a physics lesson and then asked to verbally describe the approach, the expert teachers identified larger patterns of instruction by name while the novices spoke of smaller, discrete teacher actions (Larkin, Mcdermott, Simon, & Simon, 1980). Over-contextualization, seeing something as a unique element of a specific context, rather than as one example of a larger pattern, has been identified as a key constraint for transfer of new learning (Bjork & Richardson-Klavhen, 1989). A common lexicon can reduce over-contextualization in that it supports identification of patterns of effective instructional practice, rather than isolated, individual instances.

The Artisan Teacher: A Field Guide to Skillful Teaching is an attempt to identify and organize observed patterns of skillful instruction into a common, professional lexicon that can support the development of teachers and teaching.

I should clarify here, that the field guide is a construction of my own mind. The twenty-three themes represent my best attempt at a cogent and comprehensive treatment of the patterns of successful teaching observed by me, in my career as a teacher and a developer of teachers. It is subject to the biases and misunderstandings that any one observer, however diligent, most probably commits. This work is not a peer-reviewed lexicon of instructional techniques that represents a consensus of the finest minds that ever observed a classroom. It is, rather, more like a field guide that catalogs beautiful birds, written by a single bird lover, an enthusiast, who has spent many hours in the forest looking for and at birds.

The artisan themes are derived from thousands of classroom observations. Many, even most, of the teachers who were observed were chosen based on a recommendation from their principal. I asked principals to steer me toward three or four of their most successful teachers; teachers who excelled in creativity, innovation, classroom technique, classroom climate, test scores, and parent/student satisfaction. Not every principal knows who their most successful teachers are and some get it very wrong, in my opinion. But, mostly, they get it right. And, over the years they have provided me with a buffet of great teaching to observe and study. Inside the classroom I looked for instances of instruction that resulted in unusually high levels of student engagement, success, effort, clarity, thinking, and performance. I watched for instructional approaches that increased students' speed of learning, recall of content, and transfer of knowledge and skills to new settings. When I saw these things happening, I took close and copious notes on the details of how it was happening. If I saw similar instructional results again and again, I began to craft a description of the instructional approach that most dependably delivered the positive learning results. These descriptions began to sort together as themes and the ones that recurred most often and most dependably became the twenty-three themes contained in this field guide.

Why twenty-three? I honestly wish it had worked out to a more compelling number. Ten would have been nice, or twelve. I've always liked the number eight because it has an elegant symmetry to it, I think. Twenty-one has a nice ring to it. There are twenty-three themes because that is the number of different patterns that had, in my way of thinking, substantially recurring evidence. There are twenty-three themes in the field guide because that number seemed to me to be the number that best described the patterns of successful teaching that I was repeatedly seeing.

The field guide is not intended to be an exhaustive list of all the ways teachers are excellent, but rather a useful way of looking at some of the themes that are most common and have the broadest utility. I have also noticed that successful teachers often have idiosyncratic skills; skills that are theirs alone and are not widely seen in other classrooms. It is intriguing to watch teachers use their "signature moves" at key moments of a lesson. This field guide does not attempt to describe these personal techniques since they are, by definition, not widespread. So, to be included in the field guide, a theme had to qualify in these four ways:

1. The theme must have utility in all content areas.
2. The theme must have utility for all ages and grade levels.

3. The theme must have a body of research and literature to support it.

4. The theme has to be observed repeatedly in the classrooms of successful teachers.

It is important to note that, in my observations of successful teachers, no one attempts to employ all twenty-three themes on a regular basis and certainly not in a single lesson. To do so would be counterproductive. Instead, Artisan Teachers tend to identify the themes in which they are already skilled and employ those skills first and most often, to the great benefit of their students.

Marcus Buckingham and Donald O. Clifton, in their excellent book *Now Discover Your Strengths,* describe how peak performers in every field approach their craft… "they capitalize on their strengths and manage around their weaknesses" (Buckingham & Clifton, 2001, p. 27). I see artisan teachers taking a similar approach. Instead of obsessing on areas where they are less effective, they identify their key skills, both innate and learned, and lean more heavily on those. They don't ignore their weaknesses, but rather, seek to manage them. *The Artisan Teacher: A Field Guide to Skillful Teaching* is designed to support and enhance this process. Each of the twenty-three themes is presented in an easy to access format that will enable teachers to quickly recognize the themes in their own teaching, determine key skills and strengths, and enhance their practice. Administrators and others with a role in the development of teachers can use the field guide as a resource to support growth-evoking feedback and coaching.

I'd like to gratefully acknowledge the thousands of teachers, who in the midst of a thousand busy days, welcomed me and our observation teams into their classrooms and provided both the inspiration and the evidence for the twenty-three artisan themes. You have been and will continue to be the object of my incurable fascination with excellent teaching.

How To Use This Field Guide

As with all field guides, whether for birds, insects, or wine varieties, this one is organized around topics; in this case twenty-three topics, or themes, of skillful teaching. The themes are arranged in three categories, according to the three aspects of artisanship... artisan as worker, artisan as scientist, and artisan as artist. Other than these three categories, the themes are not arranged in any other specific way. The themes are not sequential and no theme is a prerequisite for the understanding of other themes. There is, however, an underlying structure to the arrangement to the twenty-three themes that supports these approaches.

Read the Field Guide from Front to Back

All the themes are important and represent the best work of countless skillful teachers. As an overview, *The Artisan Teacher: A Field Guide to Skillful Teaching* provides a comprehensive look at many of the most common elements of successful teaching.

Read the Field Guide by Artisan Category

Artisans are skilled workers, curious scientists, and creative artists. The first six themes speak to the fundamental work of teaching. The next twelve describe the science of teaching, and the last five seek to capture the artistic nature of teaching.

Read the Field Guide by Interest

Scan the twenty-three titles and their short descriptions and start with the ones that capture your attention or imagination. Some of the twenty-three themes will likely affirm your own teaching practices and some will represent new approaches that would complement your current practices.

Read the Field Guide by Skill Type

If you're most interested in how content knowledge contributes to teaching success, go first to Clear Learning Goals, Congruency, Task Analysis, or Chunking. If you're most interested in accelerating learning for students, read Personal Relevance, Mental Models, Local Memory, or Connection. If you're curious about assessment ideas, check out Overt Responses and Performance Feedback. Enriched Environments, Success, Neural Downshifting, and Personal Presence all speak to how skillful teachers enhance the affective domain of their classrooms. If you'd like to increase student's recall skills, read Practice, First-Time Learning, or Locale Memory. And classroom management ideas can be found in Conscious Attention, Chunking, Stagecraft, or Time and Timing.

Within each theme, the reader will find a consistent set of elements that are designed to provide access to the themes at progressively greater levels of detail. Each theme chapter contains:

1. A title and short definition that promote quick identification of the theme.

2. An image that captures the essence of the theme pictorially.

3. An elaborative description that further clarifies the definition, describes key ideas from the research and literature on the theme, and provides classroom examples to clarify the concepts.

4. An online appendix of school and classroom scenarios from various grade levels and subject areas to promote further understanding and to support the reader's initial application ideas. This appendix is available at www.rutherfordlg.com.

5. An online appendix containing additional research studies, books, articles, and other suggested resources. This appendix is available at www.rutherfordlg.com.

Twenty-three of anything can feel overwhelming. Remember that the ***Artisan Teacher Field Guide*** is not a list of twenty-three things all teachers should do. It is a list of twenty-three themes of skillful teaching gleaned from thousands of teachers' classrooms. No individual teacher could or should use all of them. The most successful teachers, in my experience, capitalize on the themes where they are already most skilled, enhancing their craft in these key areas. Then, they augment and complement their instructional strengths with a few of the other themes that best fit their key strengths.

It is my hope that *The Artisan Teacher: A Field Guide to Skillful Teaching* will serve as a valuable and easy to navigate resource for teachers and teacher developers. It is offered as both a professional learning tool and also as recognition of the excellent teaching that exists in our classrooms. The field guide's most important purpose is to support the development of ever more skillful teaching… from good to great, and from great to unforgettable.

The Twenty-three Themes

An artisan is one skilled in the applied arts, a craftsperson... a unique combination of artist, scientist, and skilled laborer.

Themes that describe the **technical work** *of teaching:*

Clear Learning Goals. The ability of the teacher to identify and precisely express what students will know and be able to do as a result of a lesson.

Congruency. The ability of the teacher to design classroom activities that are accurately matched to clear learning goals.

Task Analysis. The ability of the teacher to identify and sequence all the essential steps necessary for mastery of a learning goal.

Diagnosis. The ability of the teacher to verify what students already know and can do for the purpose of determining where to begin instruction.

Overt Responses. The ability of the teacher to regularly obtain evidence of student learning for the purpose of determining next steps for teaching/learning.

Mid-Course Corrections. The ability of the teacher to quickly adapt instruction to meet learning needs based on overt student responses.

Themes that describe the **scientific aspects** *of teaching:*

Conscious Attention. The ability of the teacher to gain and then focus students' attention on a relevant learning activity.

Chunking. The ability of the teacher to segment the curriculum and learning activities into manageable portions to avoid working memory overload.

Connection. The ability of the teacher to establish a mental link between the intended learning and past learning or experiences.

Practice. The ability of the teacher to improve recall and application of learning through effective rehearsal, repeated effort, drill, repetition, study, and review

Personal Relevance. The ability of the teacher to embed the intended curriculum into issues and contexts that are linked to students' survival or immediate well being.

Locale Memory. The ability of the teacher to enhance learning by organizing information around the learner's position or "locale" in three-dimensional space.

Mental Models. The ability of the teacher to create a structure for learning using images, models, sensory experiences, symbol systems, and creative processing methodologies.

First Time Learning. The ability of the teacher to capitalize on the brain's tendency to attend to, process deeply, and recall information that is presented as new, original, or as an initial experience.

Neural Downshifting. The ability of the teacher to reduce stress and threat in the classroom environment to avoid "survival mode" thinking and to increase higher order thinking.

Enriched Environments. The ability of the teacher to shape the physical and social environment of the classroom to enhance learning.

Success. The ability of the teacher to increase and sustain student effort by designing and adapting learning tasks to ensure that students experience success.

Performance Feedback. The ability of the teacher to increase students' persistence at a task by providing knowledge of results regarding students' work.

Themes that describe the* artistic nature *of teaching:

Stagecraft. The ability of the teacher to enhance, deepen, or prolong student engagement by utilizing a theatrical treatment.

Complementary Elements. The ability of the teacher to sequence instructional experiences that build on the preceding and set the stage for the subsequent.

Time and Timing. The ability of the teacher to strategically manage the duration of learning activities and the intervals between instructional elements in order to optimize learning.

Personal Presence. The ability of the teacher to become a person of significance in the lives of students and to use this position to enhance student engagement.

Delight. The ability of the teacher to create instances of learning that are extra-memorable by designing a "positive surprise"- something that is exceptionally pleasing and unexpected.

THEME 1

Clear Learning Goals

The purpose of art is washing the dust of daily life off our souls.

– Pablo Picasso

Clear Learning Goals

Definition. The ability of the teacher to identify and precisely express what students will know and be able to do as a result of a lesson.

Elaboration. Goals can be powerful motivators. Whether one's aim is to shed a few pounds, clean out a garage, or finish an advanced degree, the act of thinking clearly about a desired outcome makes its accomplishment more likely. The author and management consultant Stephen Covey, in his best-selling book, ***The 7 Habits of Highly Effective People***, emphasized the practice of writing a personal mission statement, a set of life goals, as a key to personal effectiveness. Habit number 2, of the seven habits, is "Begin with the End in Mind" (Covey, 1989, p. 95). Covey writes "Begin with the end in mind is based on the principle that all things are created twice. There's a mental or first creation, and a physical or second creation to all things" (Covey, 1989, p. 99). Covey would go on to insist that there is something extra clarifying about the writing down of one's goals. Through the process of actually choosing nouns, verbs, tenses, and modifiers we see our goals more clearly and this added clarity is motivating, even exhilarating.

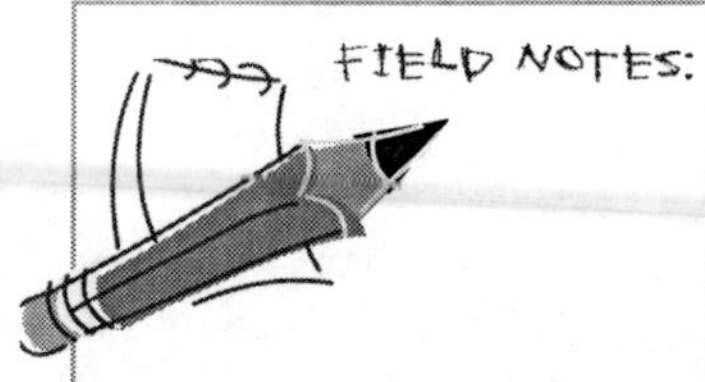

Through the process of actually choosing nouns, verbs, tenses, and modifiers we see our goals more clearly and this added clarity is motivating, even exhilarating.

"Writing or reviewing a personal mission statement changes you because if forces you to think through your priorities deeply, carefully, and to align your behavior with your beliefs" (Covey, 1989, p. 129).

The most successful teachers, in my opinion, heed Covey's advice to "begin with the end in mind." Well before the lesson begins, they have first created it in their minds. Guided by adopted curriculum standards, they imagine clearly what they wish for students to know and be able to do by the end of the lesson. Then, they take that extra clarifying step and write it down. By committing their aims to words and choosing just the right nouns, verbs, tenses, and modifiers, they create a blueprint to both guide and inspire accomplishment.

Madeline Hunter's Instructional Theory into Practice (ITIP) model was an early educational application of effectiveness through goal setting. Hunter emphasized that teacher decisions should be guided by a clear statement of the desired learning objectives, both in terms of content and learner performance (Hunter, 1994).

In practice, teachers successfully write clear learning goals in a number of formats. Some begin the goal statement with Students Will Be Able To (SWBAT). ***"Students will be able to add fractions with unlike denominators."*** Some use The Learner Will (TLW). ***"The learner will analyze energy flow through an ecosystem."*** Some use "I can statements." ***"I can use commas correctly in my writing."*** Some pose the goal as an Essential Question (EQ). ***"How can I use figurative language to make my writing more interesting?"*** Some use language from state curriculum standards. ***"0407.3.2: Investigate different ways that organisms meet their energy needs."*** And some take care to write the goals in student friendly terms. ***"We understand that each digit in a two digit number represents amounts of tens and ones."***

The purpose of writing clear learning goals is to create a mental image (for teacher and student) of a desired future state, and then to clarify that image by specifically describing it in terms of student thinking, learning, and performance (Reeves, 2011). When goals are clarified in this way, no matter the format, both teachers and students are able to pursue the work of learning with more focus, intentionality, commitment, and motivation. And, they are better able to mark progress and make adjustments along the way.

Success principles for clear learning goals.

Clear learning goals describe student learning, not classroom activities. *"Students will complete their four color map projects."* This statement describes a classroom activity, not a learning goal. *"Students will analyze population density statistics and create a graphic map display to show differences across the state."* This goal is clearer. It speaks to the students' thinking and the performances that demonstrate learning.

Clear learning goals describe both content and performance. Typically, a goal statement expresses content as nouns and performances as verbs. An incomplete sentence, therefore, represents an incomplete goal. *"Students will diagram the four steps of the water cycle and explain how each step leads to the next."* This is a complete sentence. "Four steps of the water cycle," is not.

Begin with the end in mind.
- Steven Covey

Creativity is allowing yourself to make mistakes. Art is knowing which ones to keep.

– Scott Adams

Clear learning goals contain clear verbs. *Diagram, identify, compare, solve,* and *create* are clearer verbs than *know about, understand, appreciate,* and *cover*. Clear verbs turn invisible, cognitive processes like *understand* and *appreciate* into visible, physical expressions that can be observed and assessed (Bloom, 1956). The verb *appreciate* in "Students will *appreciate* the concept of checks and balances in the federal government." is an invisible, cognitive function. Adding "by creating a diagram of the three branches of government showing the powers of each" adds a visible, physical element that is observable and assessable. A popular and effective way to test verb clarity is to apply the "Hey Dad watch me…" test (Mager, 1984). Just place the verb after the stem, "Hey Dad watch me…" and see if it makes sense. "Hey Dad watch me diagram the functions of the three branches of government." seems more plausible than "Hey Dad, watch me appreciate democracy."

Clear learning goals pervade the lesson, not simply begin the lesson. In addition to writing and sharing a goal statement at the beginning of a lesson, teachers do well to return to the goal statement several times throughout the lesson. I've observed teachers who enhance the effects of clear goals by asking students to verbalize the goal and explain it in their own words. Others ask students to write it on top of their work, affix a learning goal sticker to their projects, pause for a goal check in the midst of a learning activity, sing the goal, or place a goal statement at each center where students will work throughout the day.

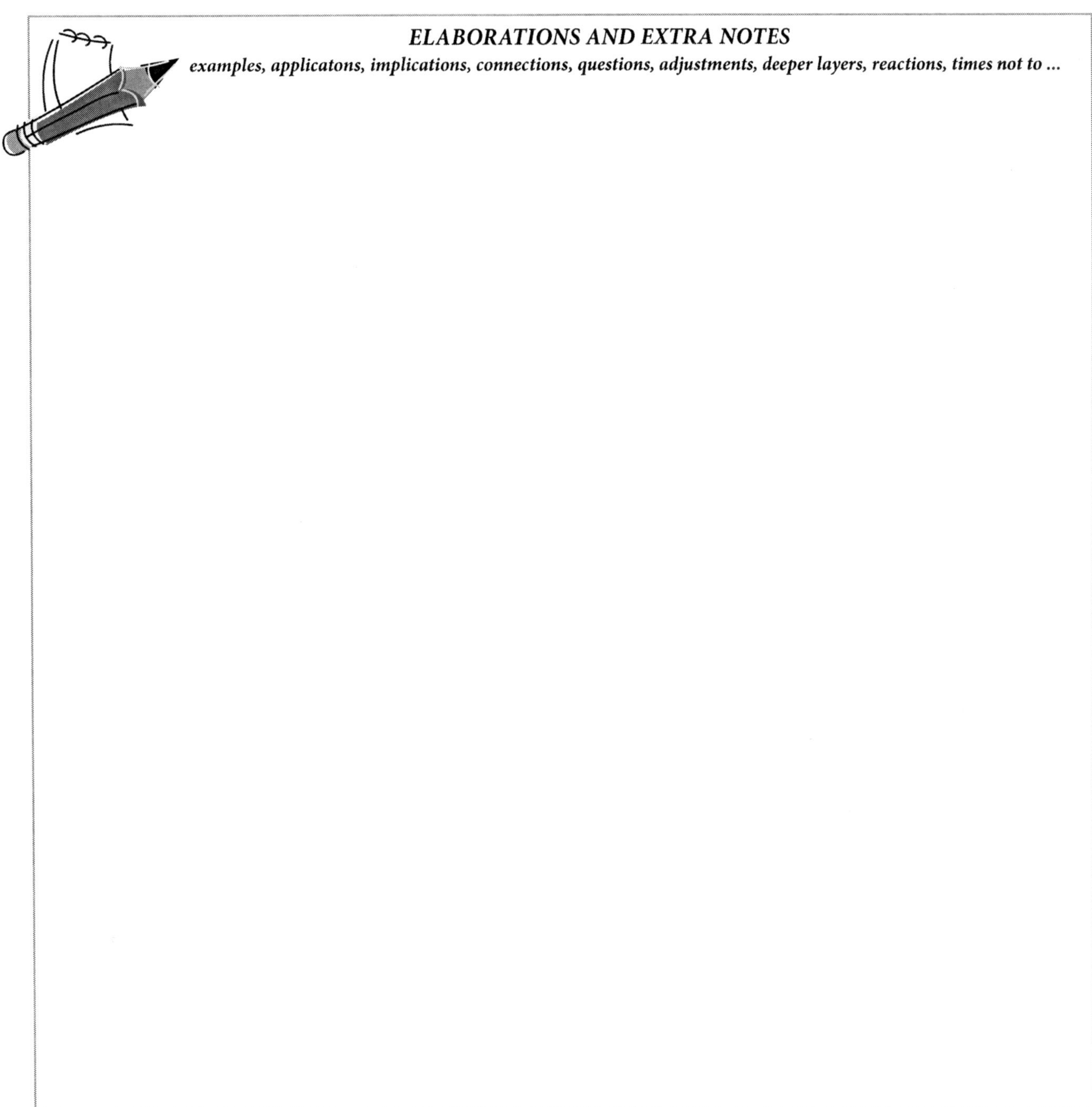

ELABORATIONS AND EXTRA NOTES

examples, applicatons, implications, connections, questions, adjustments, deeper layers, reactions, times not to ...

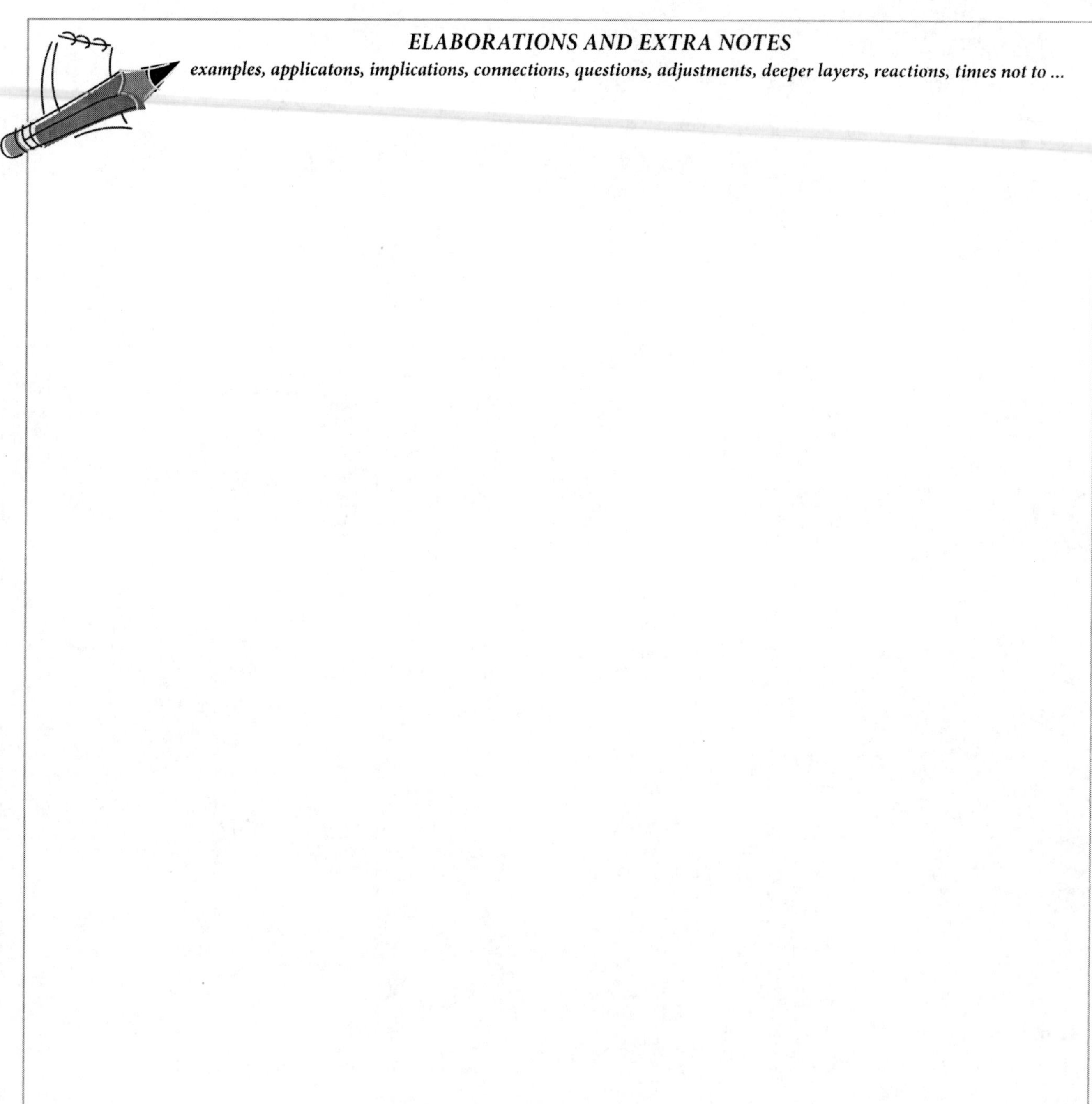
ELABORATIONS AND EXTRA NOTES
examples, applicatons, implications, connections, questions, adjustments, deeper layers, reactions, times not to ...

THEME 2

Congruency

FIELD NOTES:

It is possible to survive a day without clear goals. It is impossible, however, to survive a day with no activities!

Congruency

Definition. The ability of the teacher to design classroom activities that are accurately matched to clear learning goals.

Elaboration. Congruency is linked to, and dependent upon, clear learning goals. The essence of congruency is to match or align with something. Congruent things must have a target or another thing to which they are an exact match. Congruency is indefinable in the absence of a target. Just as one cannot give directions to an unknown destination, or dress appropriately for an unknown event, one cannot teach toward an unknown learning goal. So, by definition, congruent instructional activities cannot exist apart from a clear learning goal.

Essentially, congruency is a time management issue. The relationship between time and learning has been much studied. John Carroll made an early case for the time-learning effect in his 1963 work, *A Model for School Learning*. Carroll wrote "The learner will succeed in learning a given task to the extent that he spends the amount of time he needs to learn the task" (Carroll, 1963, p. 725). The amount of

time that students are engaged in learning has a powerful and consistent effect on the amount of learning that takes place (Walberg, 1988).

To be sure, there is much more to learning than spending enough time on it. (Kohn, 2006). "Time is a necessary, but not sufficient condition for learning. Learning takes time, but providing time does not, in itself, ensure that learning will take place" (Karweit, 1987, p.33). On balance, however, it is hard to argue that a clear eyed understanding of learning goals and the congruent activities that will most probably accomplish them are not important, even essential, skills for successful teaching. In this chapter, I'll use the term activities to stand in for all types of instructional designs, approaches, and practices.

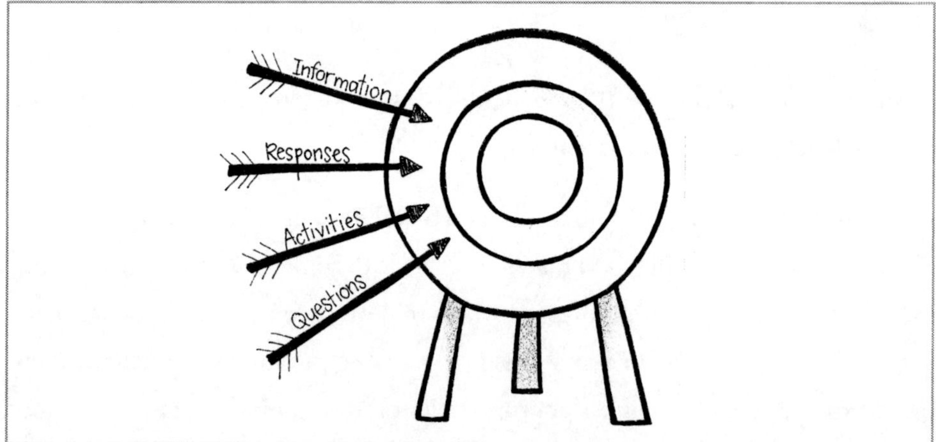

Success principles for congruency.

Goal Orientation. I've observed that classrooms seem to fall into one of two rough categories, activity-oriented or goal-oriented. In an activity-oriented classroom, the teacher plans the day as a string of activities. The activities are chosen based on their merits- what works, what the teacher likes, what matches the energy needs of the classroom, what was learned in staff development recently, what materials are available, or what other teachers have recommended. The

An education isn't how much you have committed to memory, or even how much you know. It's being able to differentiate between what you know and what you don't.

– Anatole France

activities are not necessarily off goal, but may be, at least partially, since they were selected based not on their congruency to a clear goal, but on other merits. The temptation to select activities first is strong. From a teacher's survival perspective, it is possible to survive the day without clear goals. It is impossible, however, to survive the day with no activities! In a goal-oriented classroom the teacher first develops clear learning goals, *then* chooses activities that best serve those goals based first on their congruency, and then on their other merits.

Most approaches to time management involve a clarification of one's goals, and then a detailed plan designed to accomplish the goals (Covey, 1989). Notice the sequence. It is *first*, establish goals, *then*, determine activities. This makes sense for instructional planning too. Once a clear learning goal (see Chapter 1, Clear Learning Goals, for more information) is established, congruency speaks to the ability of the teacher to match classroom resources and approaches to the goal. First, determine learning goals. Then, choose activities that serve the goals. Activities serve goals, not the other way around. This is the essence of goal orientation.

Stick-to-it-ive-ness. Teaching is not for the easily thwarted. Every day in every classroom, there are multiple opportunities to get sidetracked. There are interruptions, emergencies, announcements, attention deficits, family issues, personal issues, administrative issues, technology issues, and just plain fatigue. In and through all this, the teacher who can keep her eyes on the goal and simply stick with it, or at least keep coming back to it, serves her students well.

Discernment. Some teachers have a knack, a gift really, for quickly recognizing a potential activity's level of congruency. They can spot incongruent activities quickly, identify which parts of an activity are congruent and which are not, and can avoid being fooled by an activity's other merits. The key skill here is the ability to *discern* (distinguish between) classroom activities that are *congruent* (an exact

Every artist was first an amateur.

– Ralph Waldo Emerson

Art is not a thing;
it is a way.
– Elbert Hubbard

match to the goal) from those which are merely *correlated* (has some relationship to the goal).

A discerning 9th grade science teacher worries that the time her students are spending on projects for the school's annual science fair isn't delivering a big enough return on their investment. Often, the experimental elements are accomplished rather quickly and the concepts mastered soon thereafter. Then, lots of time is spent coloring, cutting, pasting, decorating, and displaying the experiment in order to impress the judges. The discerning teacher decides that the experimental and concept mastery work is congruent to the class's learning goals, but that the work of decorating and displaying the results is only correlated.

The 2nd grade teacher states this learning goal: *I can explain how illustrations support a text and help to create a mood. RL.3.7.* The first activity asks students to view various illustrations from favorite books and describe the mood that each illustration evokes. They volunteer "sad," "scary," and "funny" to describe the moods they feel for each illustration. "Pretty good" the teacher thinks to herself, "but this only addresses part of the goal. I have to find some way to have them explain how the illustrations support the text." She then asks students to read short, un-illustrated text excerpts and describe the moods they feel after each reading. They volunteer "suspenseful," "joyful," and "surprised." Next, she posts the mood words from both exercises on a big board and asks students to arrange illustrations and text excerpts around the mood words that each illustration or text excerpt best fits, showing the connections with yarn and push pins. The visual representation that emerges shows how illustrations are linked to moods and how illustrations, through the moods they evoke, can support the text. "That's pretty close" the teacher thinks as she discerns the match between the goal and her activities.

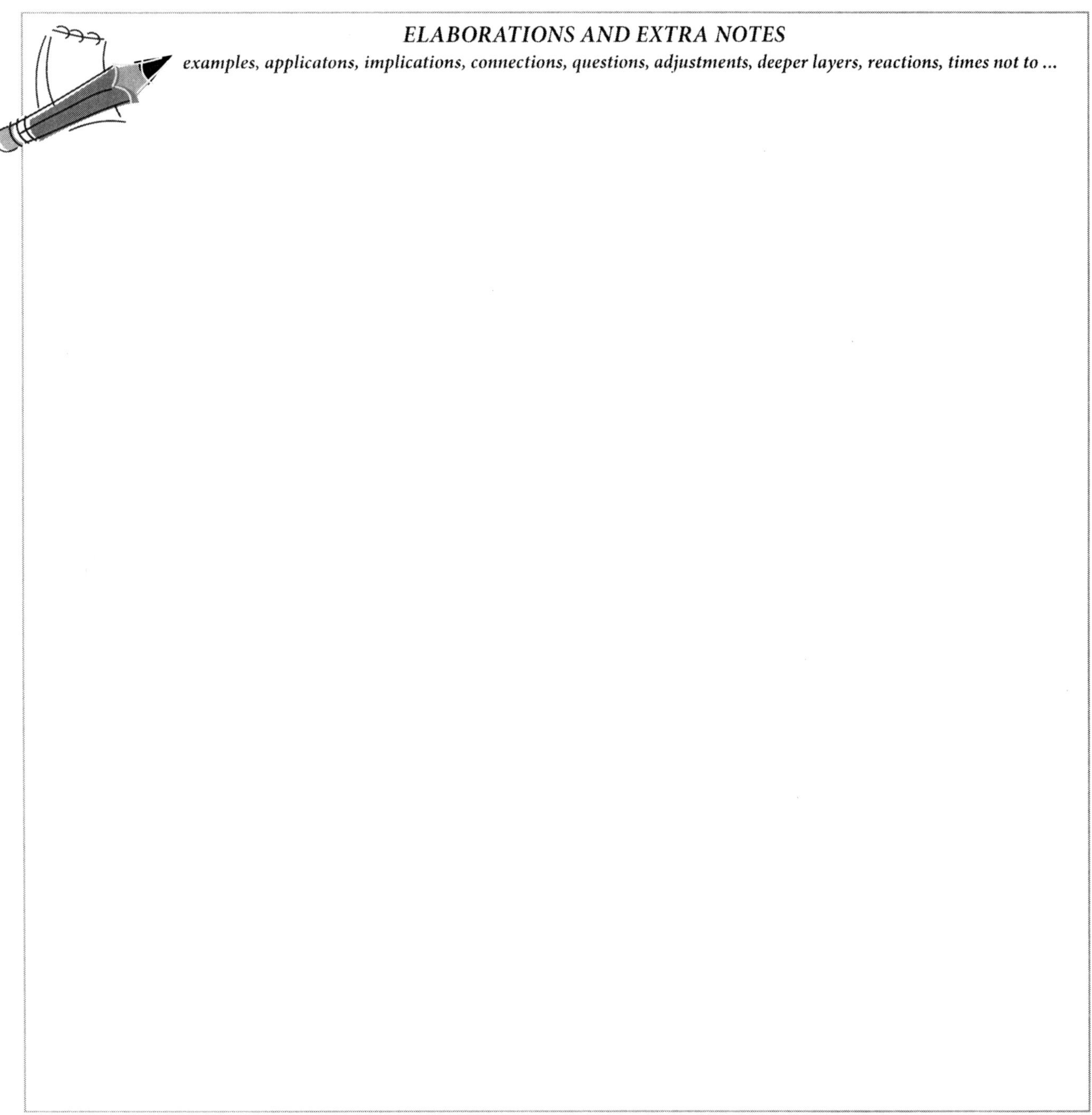

ELABORATIONS AND EXTRA NOTES

examples, applicatons, implications, connections, questions, adjustments, deeper layers, reactions, times not to ...

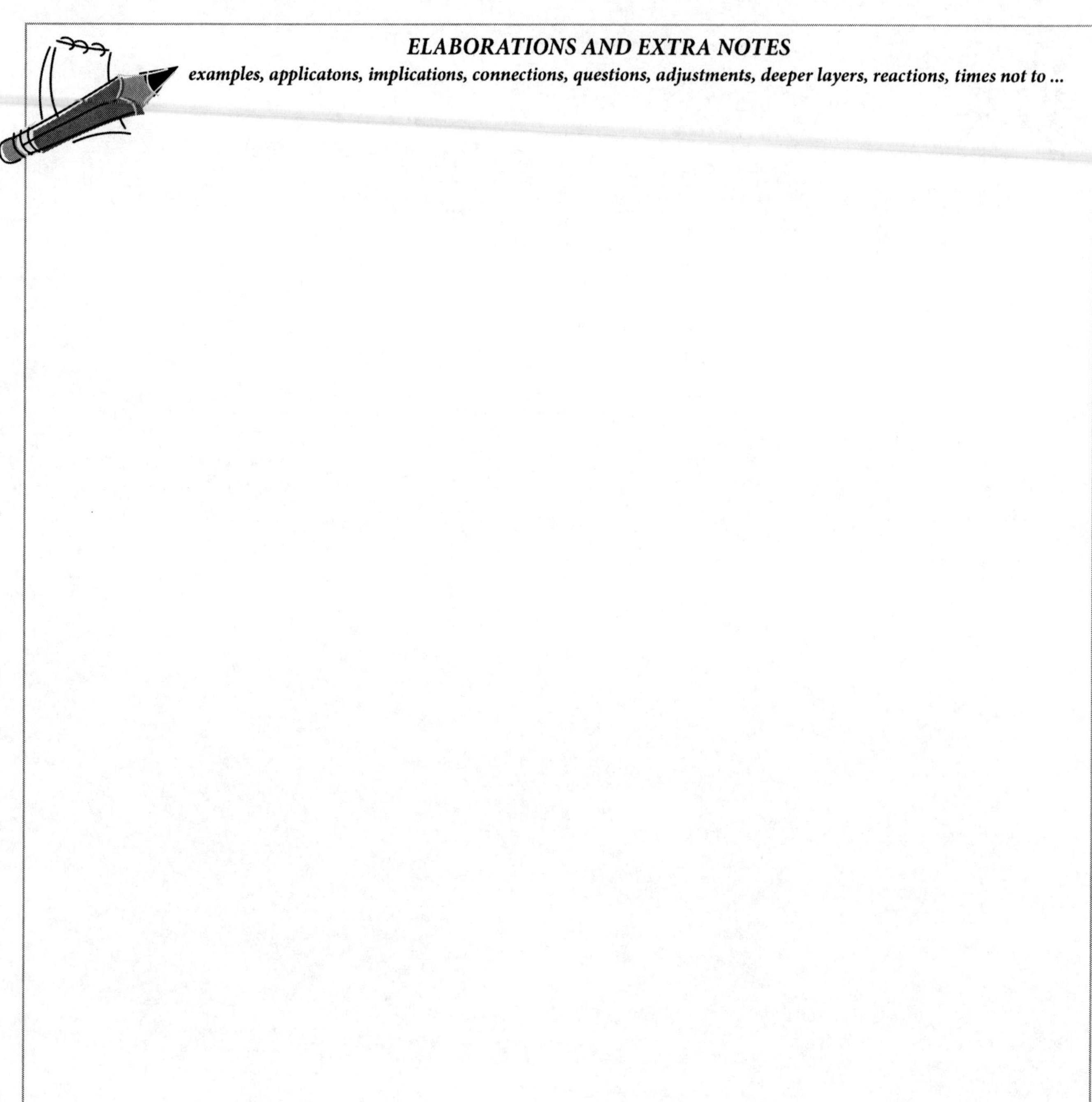

ELABORATIONS AND EXTRA NOTES

examples, applicatons, implications, connections, questions, adjustments, deeper layers, reactions, times not to ...

THEME 3

Task Analysis

FIELD NOTES:

The roots of education are bitter, but the fruit is sweet.

- Aristotle

Task Analysis

Definition. The ability of the teacher to identify and sequence the essential steps necessary for mastery of a learning goal.

Elaboration. Any complex and important act merits a thorough thinking through before one commences to action, especially in cases where failure is unacceptable or not easily corrected. This thinking through process is called a task analysis.

An airline pilot files a flight plan that details the flight, destination, waypoints, route, altitude, and passenger list. Before departure though, the pilot goes through a pre-flight checklist to ensure that the aircraft is safe and able to fly. The checklist includes all the major systems on the aircraft and is designed to be performed in a prescribed sequence. This is a task analysis.

An architect creates a blueprint from which a home will be built, but it is the construction plan, developed after the blueprint, that specifies exactly what will be done and in what sequence to stay on schedule and to minimize costs. The site must be cleared of trees before construction can begin. While the expensive

Every artist dips his brush in his own soul, and paints his own nature into his pictures.

– Henry Ward Beecher

grading equipment is on site, it makes sense to dig the sewer and utility trenches right away, even though they won't be needed until later in the project. The construction manager understands this and schedules the heavy equipment accordingly. The construction plan calls for all the masonry work to be completed on consecutive days, even though the brickwork doesn't hold up other tasks and could be done in segments. As it turns out, because of a positive learning curve (Thomas, Matthews, & Ward, 1986), masons will complete the brickwork in less time, at a lower cost, and with higher quality workmanship if they are not interrupted, but rather can complete the entire façade of the building in consecutive days. The construction manager understands the interplay of all these variables and plans accordingly (Baker, 1974). This is a task analysis.

The character Sherlock Holmes noted "Most people, if you describe a train of events to them, will tell you what the result would be. They can put those events together in their minds, and argue that something will come to pass. There are a few people, however, who, if you told them a result, would be able to evolve from their own inner consciousness what the steps were that led up to that result. This power is what I mean when I talk of reasoning backward." (Doyle, 1930, p.83).

Teachers are kindred souls to pilots, constructional managers, and detectives. When they examine learning goals carefully and plan for the exact sequence of cognitive, physical, or affective experiences that will engender optimal learning for their students, they are using task analysis to ensure success. Task analysis is called for, both inside and outside of education, when stakes are high, failure is especially costly, and when there is complex interplay among the variables for success (Gagne, 1963).

We don't perform pre-drive checklists before driving to the corner store. If the car dies, we'll just call for help. A construction plan is not needed for adding a bookshelf to one's office and we need not involve Sherlock Holmes to solve a

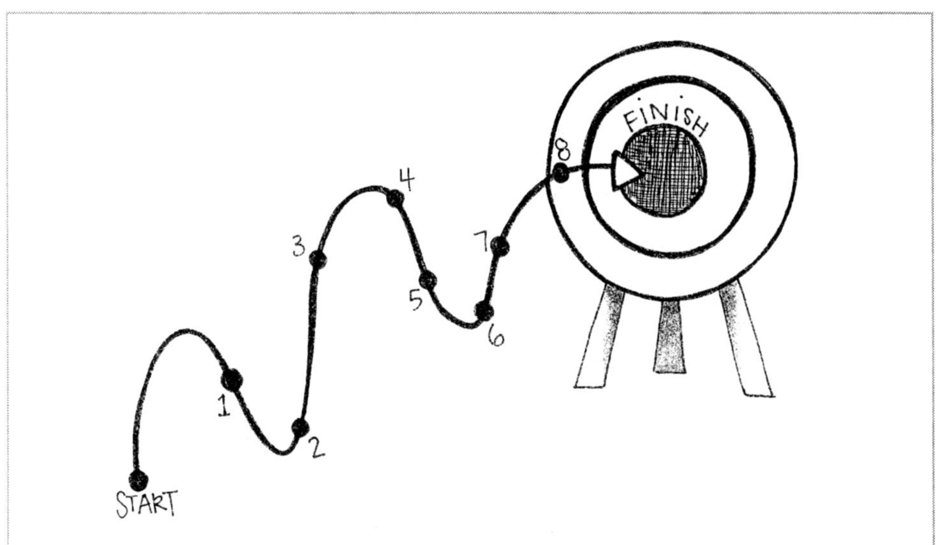

convenience store robbery. Likewise, not every episode of instruction requires a task analysis. Some, maybe even most, learning goals are straightforward and uncomplicated. Task analysis is called for when planning key, important concepts that will serve as the foundation for much future learning, when learning goals are more complex and intertwined, and/or when students have historically shown a wide achievement gap. When learning goals are complex, it is easy to overlook key steps. (Jonassen, Tessmer & Hannum, 1999) refer to task analysis as a blueprint for instruction. "Without the blueprint, important parts of the lesson may be ignored, or the components and activities may not support each other" (Jonessen, et.al., 1999, p. vii). Arlin (1984) details how students have multiple opportunities to fail when the curriculum is complex and each step builds on the assumption of mastery of previous steps. "A student who begins a learning sequence by performing poorly on the first step performs even more poorly on the second step because he lacks some of the prerequisites. Without extra time to restudy these prerequisites, he misses more prerequisites at each successive step, becoming progressively farther behind. So the academically rich get richer and the academically poor get poorer" (Arlin, 1984, p.67).

Teachers are kindred souls to pilots, construction managers, and detectives.

He who opens a school door, closes a prison.

– Victor Hugo

Success principles for task analysis.

Task analysis is a 3 step process: First, establish a clear learning goal (see Chapter 1). A task analysis cannot, by definition, be developed without a clear aiming point or predetermined result. Second, list all the essential sub-learnings that are necessary for mastery of the learning goal. Don't worry about sequence at this point, just list everything that a learner needs to know and be able to do to master the stated learning goal. For example, if the learning goal is: *Students will be able to add fractions with unlike denominators.* Then the list would include, identifying numerators and denominators, finding the greatest common factor, finding the least common denominator, writing complex numbers as improper fractions, etc. Step 3: Sequence the sub-learnings. Look at the list and decide which should come first, then second, then third, etc. Sometimes this decision will be straightforward because the content contains dependent sequences. Multiplication must precede division. One must master the concept of verbs before one attempts adverbs and gerunds. Sometimes the content is not sequentially dependent. When one learns the three additive primary colors, it does not matter if the sequence is red, yellow, blue or blue, red, yellow, just so they are all included. In this case, a sequence still needs to be determined, but it can be based on other considerations.

Include only essential sub-learnings. A task analysis is not a list of all the things that *might* be included in a lesson sequence. It is a list of all the things that *must* be included. A task analysis is best viewed as a lean construct, containing only those items that are absolutely essential for mastery of the leaning goal. When learning to swim, one might as well learn to float also. But floating would not be included in the task analysis for swimming because it is not essential. One can learn to swim without learning how to float.

Include sub-learnings, not activities. A task analysis is a sequenced list of essential sub-learnings, not a list of activities. If activities are allowed to be a part of a task analysis, the door is open to learners successfully completing the activities, but not mastering the learning. Using the example of swimming again, if the goal is to learn to swim using the crawl stroke, then "learning to flutter kick" might be one of the essential sub-learnings. The activity "kick-boarding," using a small foam board to keep the upper body afloat so the swimmer can isolate and improve kicking technique, might be a good way to teach the flutter kick, but it would not appear on a task analysis. It is an activity, not a sub-learning. It is possible to do well with kick-boarding, but still not learn the flutter kick. A task analysis is a sequenced list of essential sub-learnings, not a list of activities.

Develop task analyses collaboratively. A task analysis, since it involves some complexity and judgment is best developed by a team of teachers. No one teacher likely knows all the steps or has anticipated all the twists and turns in a learning sequence. With respect to task analysis, two heads, or better yet five or six, are better than one.

The illiterate of the future will not be the person who cannot read. It will be the person who does not know how to learn.

– Alvin Toffler

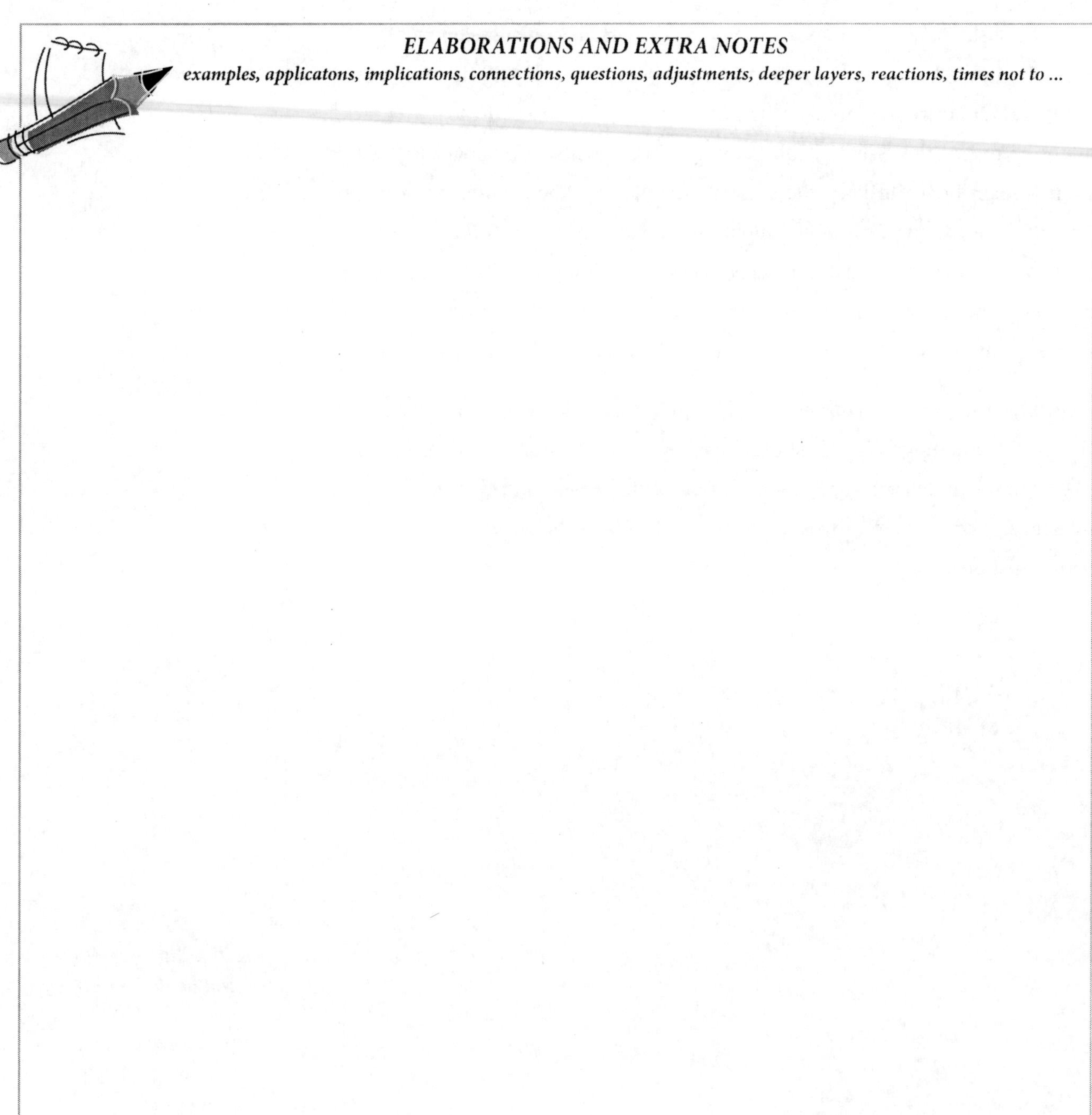

ELABORATIONS AND EXTRA NOTES

examples, applicatons, implications, connections, questions, adjustments, deeper layers, reactions, times not to ...

THEME 4

Diagnosis

FIELD NOTES:

It is a physician's, and a teacher's, informal diagnosis skills, however, that are most prized.

Diagnosis

Definition. The ability of the teacher to verify what students already know and can do for the purpose of determining where to begin instruction.

Elaboration. Formative assessment can be defined as the frequent, interactive evoking of evidence of student progress and understanding which can be used as feedback to adjust teaching and learning (Black & William, 1998). For the purpose of *The Artisan Teacher: A Field Guide to Skillful Teaching*, which is to identify and explore common, recurring themes of skillful teaching, it seems helpful to divide this important aspect of teaching into two themes. I'll call formative assessment that occurs prior to the commencement of a lesson, for the purpose of determining where to begin instruction, *Diagnosis*, (this chapter, 4). Formative assessment that occurs during instruction, for the purpose of determining adjustments and next steps, will be called *Overt Responses* (see chapter 5). The techniques and approaches observed as teachers successfully employ diagnosis and overt responses are similar, and in some respects identical. The difference between the two, and the reason for dividing these skill patterns into two themes,

is timing and purpose. Diagnosis elicits evidence of learning for the purpose of choosing the best starting point for a lesson. Overt responses are elicited for the purpose of adjusting instruction in the midst of the lesson.

Diagnosis is often used as a medical term and understanding it as such provides a helpful perspective. Much time in a physician's education and training is spent developing diagnostic skills. Swelling, a rash, but no fever indicates an allergic reaction, but localized swelling and redness might indicate an insect bite instead. The physician is trained to gather and interpret evidence. To gather the needed evidence, the physician uses techniques that make the invisible, inner workings of the body, apparent, visible, and measurable. Physicians, and educators, rely on three types (levels, depths) of diagnosis: formal, informal and inferential.

Formal diagnosis involves a thorough and extensive battery of tests and measurements. A thorough yearly "physical" is an example. Based on these results, a patient's overall health can be determined and also areas of concern. Formal classroom diagnosis, similarly, involves batteries of tests and assessments which provide a comprehensive, albeit expensive and time consuming, look at a students' overall academic fitness.

Informal diagnosis involves a quick check of specific evidence to address a specific ailment. After thirty minutes in the doctor's office, we leave with a prescription and feel better in a few days. In the classroom, teachers use informal diagnosis to gather and interpret a quick sample of student work that relates directly to the upcoming learning task.

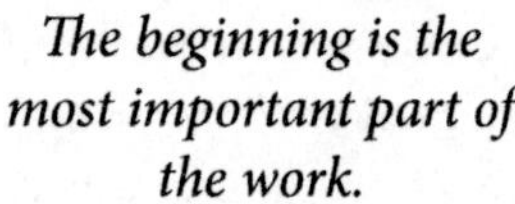

The beginning is the most important part of the work.

– Plato

Inferential diagnosis is not based on any direct evidence, but on the doctor's educated guess. The doctor might infer "Let's see... it's February and you're an elementary school teacher. I'm guessing you caught the flu from one of your students." A teacher might infer "We're two months into this biology course, so you should probably know about chromosomes and genes, but you're probably not yet familiar with Punnett squares. So, that's where we'll start today." Inferential diagnosis, in medicine or education, is fast, but risky, and often inaccurate.

In medicine and education, all three types of diagnosis have their place. It is a physician's, and a teacher's, *informal diagnosis* skills, however, that are most prized. Skilled practitioners have techniques for quickly eliciting key information from their patients (students) and using that information to design treatments (lessons) that are "just what the doctor ordered."

Before commencing a unit on mammals, a third grade teacher uses a KWL chart (a three column list of what students already know, what they wish to know, and what they learned in the lesson) to list things that students already know about mammals and what they want to know. As the students volunteer information, the teacher listens, probes, and follows up with each response in order to interpret the class's prior knowledge (Ciofalo & Wylie, 2006). This ten minute informal diagnosis gets the students thinking in the right direction and also provides the teacher with information needed to determine the best starting point for the lesson.

The U.S. History teacher passes out a five question quiz on the great depression. "Don't worry. This is not for a grade. I just want to see how much you already know about the great depression so I don't spend our valuable time teaching things you already know."

Education is simply the soul of a society as it passes from one generation to another.

– Gilbert K. Chesterton

I found I could say things with color and shapes that I couldn't say any other way - things I had no words for.

- Georgia O'Keeffe

The 2nd grade teacher uses several informal reading inventories to assess students' readiness in phonics, fluency, and vocabulary. The inventories are mostly checklists. She engages students in small groups and makes tallies on the checklists each time a student demonstrates the specific skill being assessed. After fifteen minutes or so with each reading group, the teacher scans the checklists to identify trends and themes. She plans the upcoming reading lesson accordingly.

A high school art teacher explains to his students "The human face is one of the most challenging things to sketch accurately. I'd like you to take a sheet of sketch paper and draw a human face as you see it in your mind's eye. I want you to work quickly and simply block out the major features- eyes, nose mouth, ears, and hair. You have five minutes. Go!" As the students draw, the teacher circulates around the studio to observe their work. The teacher is not only looking for how well they sketch, but for what this quick draw activity reveals about their preconceptions, or misconceptions, about the structure of the human face (Johnston, Markel, & Haley-Oliphant, 1987). After surveying their work, the teacher identifies common misunderstandings and begins the unit with the three most common misconceptions about the human face.

In each case, the teacher uses an informal diagnosis, collecting quick bits of information from students just prior to engaging them in a new, or the next, learning experience. These bits of information, though not comprehensive or complete, can, in the mind of a talented teacher, inform an interpretation of approximately where the students are. This, in turn, informs the teaching decision of where to begin the next lesson (Heritage, 2010). When teachers begin lessons at just the place students are next ready to be successful, and then keep checking and adjusting to keep instruction at or near this right place, student engagement and learning is optimized (Vygotsky, 1978, 1986; Popham, 2011).

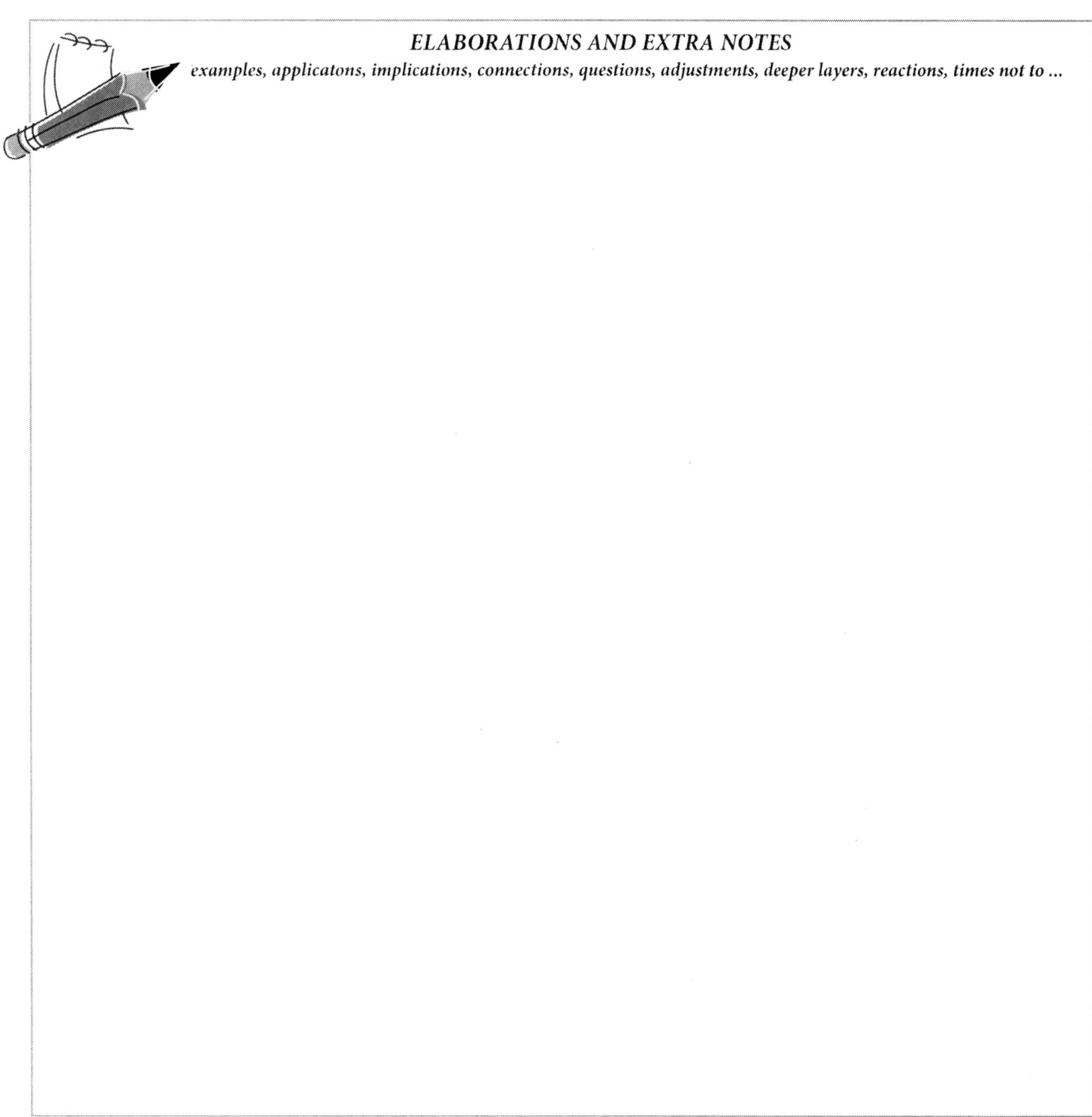

ELABORATIONS AND EXTRA NOTES

examples, applicatons, implications, connections, questions, adjustments, deeper layers, reactions, times not to ...

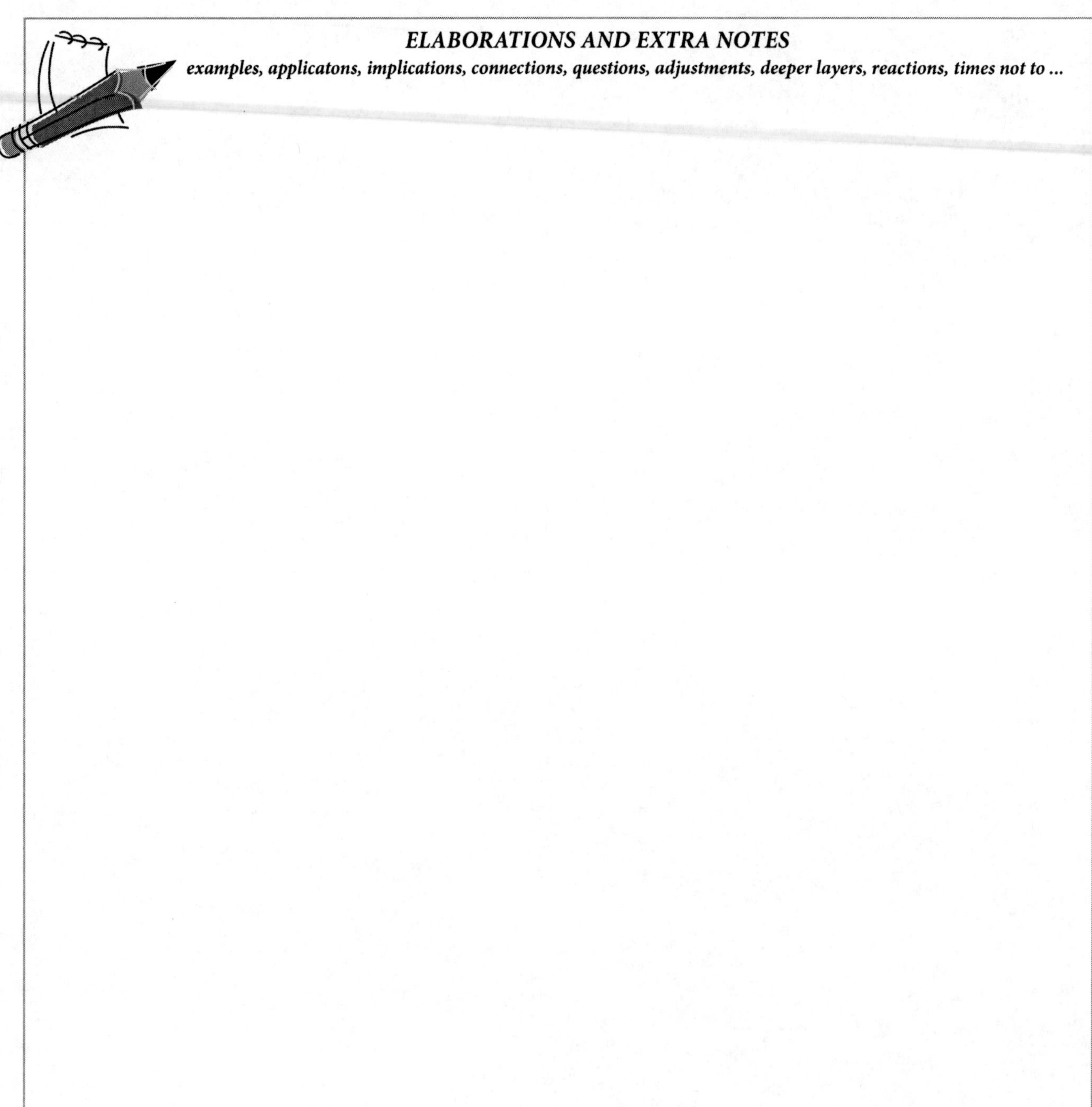
ELABORATIONS AND EXTRA NOTES
examples, applicatons, implications, connections, questions, adjustments, deeper layers, reactions, times not to ...

THEME 5

Overt Responses

Overt Responses

Definition. The ability of the teacher to regularly obtain evidence of student learning for the purpose of determining next steps for teaching.

Elaboration. Back in the "old days" of full service gas stations, the attendant would politely ask "Check the oil, sir?" I can still picture my dad popping the hood latch and responding, "Yes, please do." The attendant then reached under the hood and pulled out a long metal strip. He wiped it off and then reinserted it, waited a second, then pulled it out again. By this time my dad was usually at the attendant's side and they both looked intently at the dipstick to see the line of oil that indicated the engine's oil level. This fascinated me, that a car would have such an ingenious device as a dipstick that allowed a direct observation into the invisible inner workings of the engine. It doesn't take much to fascinate an eight year old boy, and dipsticks are not exactly high tech by today's standards, but the essential principle is timeless. *To understand, one must have a way to look inside, to make the invisible visible.*

Children have to be educated, but they have also to be left to educate themselves.

– Ernest Dimnet

Wouldn't it be great if students came equipped with dipsticks? Halfway through a math lesson a teacher could extract the dipsticks, check the levels of learning,

then make some adjustments. Of course, this is exactly what successful teachers do every day. They have ways of making the invisible, inner workings of students' minds visible.

These "ways of seeing the invisible" are called overt responses. The process is also referred to as checking for understanding, monitoring, or formative assessment. Teachers who regularly elicit overt responses from students reap benefits in two ways.

First, they gain specific and immediate information about how students are doing. This "just in time" information is critical to making immediate adjustments to instruction (Sime & Boyce, 1969).

Second, the process of eliciting overt responses promotes a more active, participative, and engaging learning environment. A classroom rich in overt responses is, by design, a classroom characterized by much active interplay among teacher and students. Research has consistently found student leaning to be enhanced by direct engagement with teachers rather than extensive reliance on individual seatwork or written assignments (Gutierrez & Slavin, 1991). Students in classrooms which rely mostly on seatwork or where students engage extensively with educational materials, rather than with the teacher and other students, are less likely to actively process new material (Walberg, 1991).

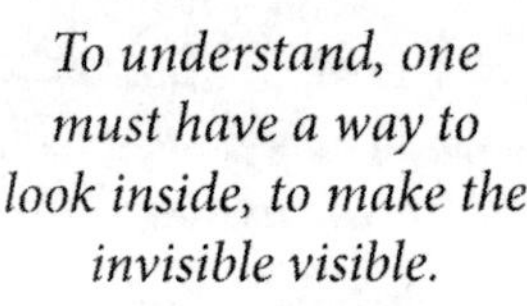

To understand, one must have a way to look inside, to make the invisible visible.

Success principles for overt responses.

Elicit overt responses from all students. This is, admittedly, a difficult standard to reach. It is, nevertheless, crucial. To elicit overt responses from less than 100% of the students is to, by design, leave the learning of some students unchecked. In statistics and survey methodology, this approach is called sampling. Sampling is "the act, process, or technique of selecting a representative part of a population for the purpose of determining parameters or characteristics of the whole population." (http://www.meriam-webster.com/dictionary/sampling). Sampling is cheaper and faster than obtaining responses from an entire population, and so it has its place as a statistical technique. It is, however, a dubious practice in the classroom, where knowledge of each individual's work is just as, if not more, important as knowledge of the class's work. Who would go to a hospital where the nursing staff only checked on every fifth patient and then planned treatments based on this statistical sample of patient's conditions? Besides the lack of information that classroom sampling provides, the practice also does not adequately deliver the second benefit of overt responses; a classroom climate of active engagement. I recall countless classroom observations where most students listen as a few students respond to the teacher's prompts or questions. These episodes of instruction were usually characterized by low energy, lack of active processing, and increasingly off task behaviors.

Another way to think about collecting overt responses from all students is to think of engagement techniques as being either mandatory or optional for students. Mandatory engagement requires overt responses. The students' level of engagement is increased through an instructional design that intentionally elicits overt responses. Mandatory engagement is a function of the teacher's design for engagement and does not rely too much on the students' cooperation or motivation. Optional engagement provides an opportunity for students to engage, but stops short of asking them to do so overtly.

Some painters transform the sun into a yellow spot, others transform a yellow spot into the sun.

- Pablo Picasso

A second grade teacher writes two numbers on the board with a blank in between. She then asks her students to think to themselves whether a >, <, or = sign should go between the numbers. After a thinking pause, the teacher says "show me" and *all* the students use their fingers to make a >,< or = sign. The teacher scans each child's hand signal and then says, "Let's do another one."

A 9th grade English teacher positions students desks in a U shape and stands in the center of the open end. Each student has a sheet of text and a yellow highlighter. The teacher asks students to highlight all the dependent clauses in the text. The teacher, knowing there are five dependent clauses in the text, and knowing the position of each on the page, can see the work of *all* students and see immediately who is correctly identifying the dependent clauses, and who is not.

Overt responses must be visible and countable. Overt engagement produces a work product that can be verified– the teacher can see it, hear it, touch it, taste it, or smell it. The art teacher says to her class, "I want you to hold up your drawing and point to your horizon line." The results here are visible. Students could decide not to hold up their drawings, but it would be obvious and evident to the teacher. In collecting overt responses, teachers look for *proof* of learning, *evidence* of thinking, and *artifacts* of performance.

Covert engagement produces a work product that is internal, mental, or hidden, such that it cannot be verified with certainty. The language arts teacher is reading a passage from a novel and asks students to imagine a scene. "Can you smell the wood fire burning? Is the wind in your face or at your back?" Students have their eyes closed and seem to be imagining something. The work is not verifiable, however. A student could choose not to engage and remain undiscovered. Overt engagement drives learning and so does covert engagement. Engagement of either type is positive and productive. The advantage of overt engagement is that it increases the probability that students will engage by making the engagement

I am often amazed at how much more capability and enthusiasm for science there is among elementary school youngsters than among college students.

– Carl Sagan

or the non-engagement visible. Not all engagement can be overt, but a healthy combination of overt and covert can greatly increase the probability of both types of engagement (Rutherford, 2009b).

Overt responses should be gathered during instruction, not following instruction. An exit slip, ticket out the door, or quiz at the end of the day are each productive strategies, but none are, by definition, overt responses. Overt responses occur *during* instruction, so that the benefits of active engagement and authentic assessment can be realized right away.

Madeline Hunter, in a presentation I attended in 1988, said something that I've always remembered because of its simplicity and poignancy. She said "You can recognize a master teacher by her pace. It's: teach – teach – check. Teach – teach – check." (Hunter, 1988). "I've got it!" I said to myself. "It's not: teach – teach – teach – teach – teach – and then, check at the end. The checking has to be right there with the teaching."

I observed a third grade teacher at the very beginning of a lesson. She began by giving directions on where the students were to go and what they were to do once the activity began. After speaking for just a moment, the teacher stopped and asked students to pair up and explain the directions so far to an imaginary new student who just joined the group. "I'll listen in to see how you do," she said. I thought to myself, "Wow! she hasn't even begun the activity and she is already checking for understanding using overt responses."

Don't just invite engagement. Plan for it. Teachers should plan their engagement strategies right along with their instructional strategies. A teacher might think, "From 10:00 a.m. till 10:15 a.m. this morning I want to review for the upcoming quiz by asking students sample questions and giving them some additional practice at answering." And also think, "I'll do this by posing a question to the

Education is what survives when what has been learned has been forgotten.
– B. F. Skinner

whole class, asking students to pause 15 seconds to think, then providing 15 more seconds for each student to write their answer on their mini white boards. Then I'll say, show me." The first thought was an *instructional* plan, the second thought was an *engagement* plan (Rutherford, 2009b).

When observing classroom instruction, I am often amazed at the high quality and rigor of questions, discussions, and activities teachers devise for students. I am frustrated though, when I notice that not all the students are engaging in the teachers' designs. It strikes me as a bit of a waste of effort and teaching talent.

So, if a book is not read, is it still a good book? If a doctor's advice is not followed, is it still good advice? In a pure sense, the answer is probably yes to both these questions. But in a practical sense, one has to wonder, "What's the point?" There is a sense of sad incompleteness when a good work, because of a lack of engagement, produces little or no result (Rutherford, 2009b). Perhaps this is why my mother demanded that I eat all the food on my plate. She said, "Children are starving in Ethiopia." I suspect what she meant was, "I invested a good bit of time and talent into the making of this meal. It would be a shame to waste it."

Education is learning what you didn't even know you didn't know.

- Daniel J. Boorstin

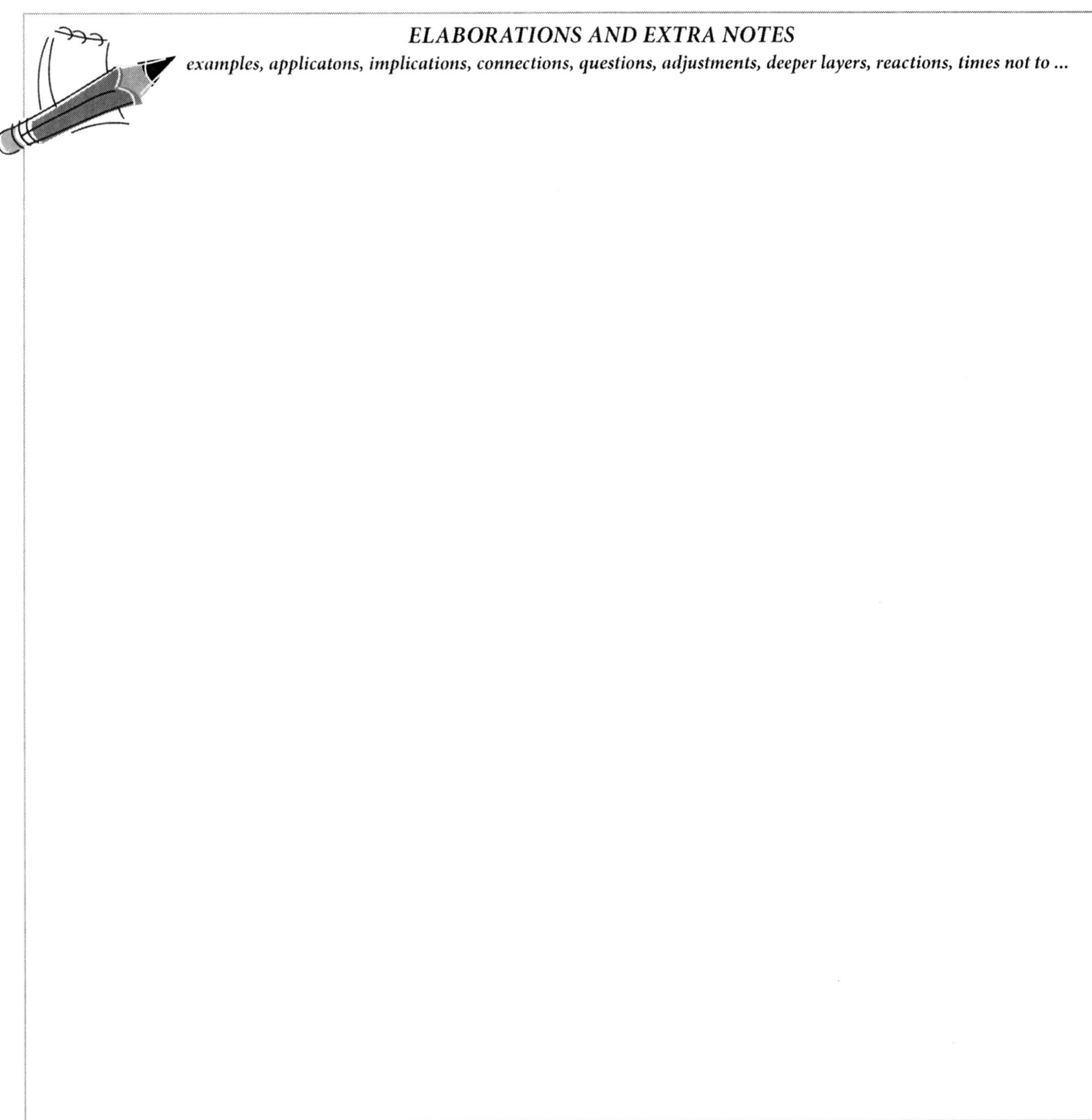

ELABORATIONS AND EXTRA NOTES

examples, applicatons, implications, connections, questions, adjustments, deeper layers, reactions, times not to ...

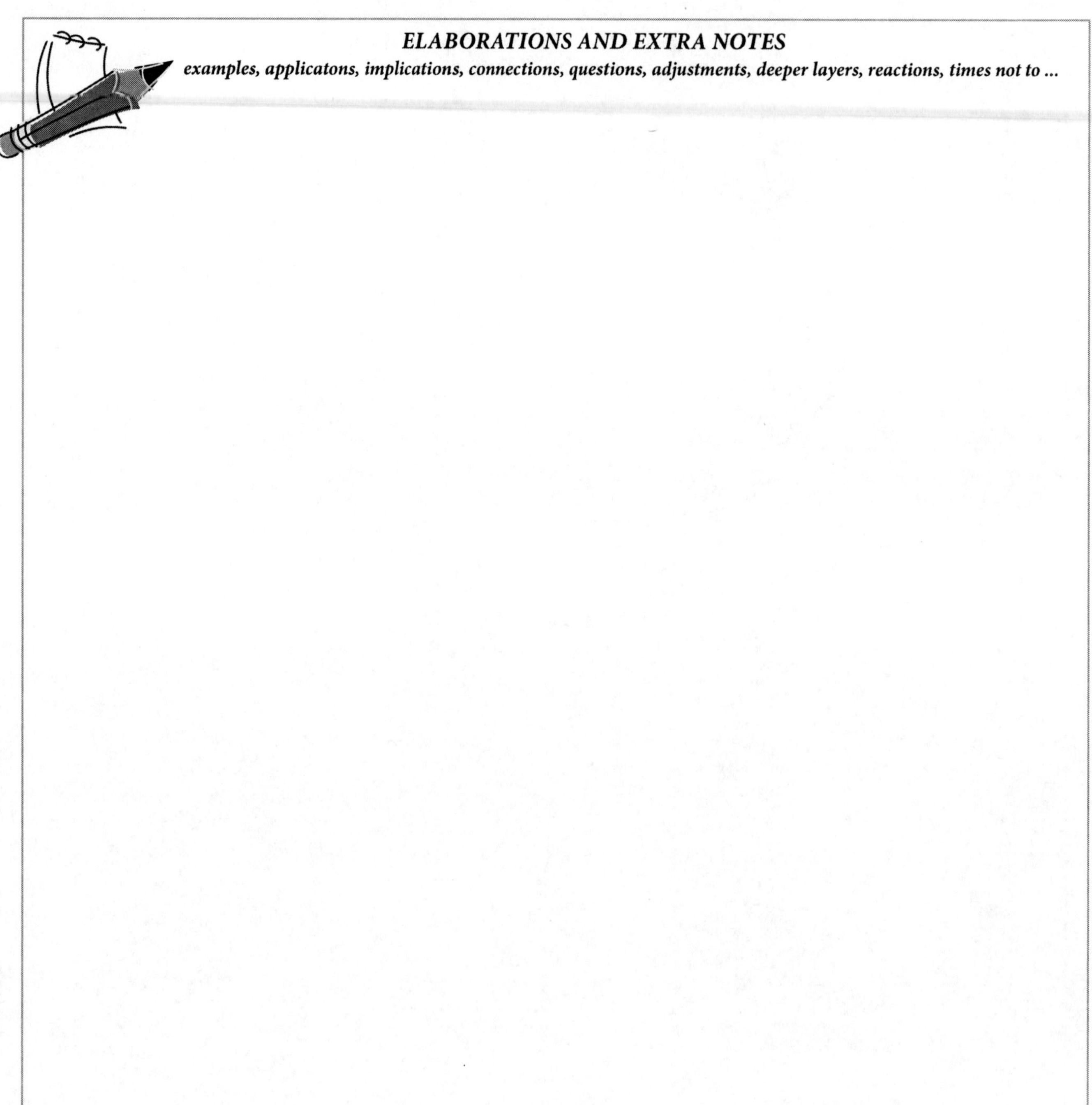
ELABORATIONS AND EXTRA NOTES
examples, applicatons, implications, connections, questions, adjustments, deeper layers, reactions, times not to ...

THEME 6

Mid-Course Corrections

Mid-Course Corrections

Definition. The ability of the teacher to quickly adapt instruction to meet students' immediate learning needs.

Elaboration. It would seem that almost every complex and wondrous creation is the product of a worthy goal and a willingness to make adjustments along the way. A novelist begins a work with a clear plan for the story, but is open to adjustments as the characters and plot unfold into words. Sometimes the best vacation memories result from spontaneous side trips or last minute changes to the itinerary.

The Apollo 11 mission to the moon involved a detailed mission plan, but also thousands of mid-course corrections. Perhaps the most famous adjustment to the plan was Neil Armstrong's manual landing of the craft after it overshot its landing point by four miles. It wasn't in the script, but Armstrong took the craft's controls, found a new landing area among boulders and craters, and deftly landed the Eagle with only sixteen seconds of fuel left in the tanks (Shepard, Slayton, & Barbee, 1994).

... mid-course corrections are not changes to the goal, but rather, changes to the steps, strategies, or activities designed to reach the goal.

The lesson from all these examples is that mid-course corrections are integral to the creative process. Note that mid-course corrections are not changes to the goal, but rather, changes to the steps, strategies, or activities designed to reach the goal. The changes are possible because of new information that is only available once the journey is underway. Mid-course corrections don't make goal setting and detailed planning obsolete. On the contrary, mid-course corrections ensure that important goals, especially lofty, complex ones, have the maximum opportunity for accomplishment.

Classroom mid-course corrections work the same way. When teachers assess student learning often and, based on what is found, make immediate adjustments to instruction, learning is optimized (Dwyer, 2008; Heritage, 2010). The window for instructional adaptation is often small. This places a premium on the teacher's ability to make changes quickly, often in the midst of an instructional sequence. Popham (2011) writes, "It is difficult to argue with the instructional virtues of immediacy; any sort of self-correcting system is certain to work better if along the way corrections are made as quickly as possible" (p. 48). It is important that formative assessment (See Chapter 5, Overt Responses) practices be embedded into instruction, not designed to follow it (William & Thompson, 2007). "Formative assessment is part of the instructional process. When incorporated into classroom practice, it provides the information needed to adjust teaching and learning *while they are happening*" (emphasis mine) (Garrison & Ehringhaus, 2007, p.1).

Mid-course corrections can take many forms. Teachers, based on their interpretation of formative assessment data, might decide to alter the pace of the lesson, use different activities or approaches, change the grouping of students, change the level of materials, or any other combination of adjustments. Here, in no particular order, are six common types of mid-course corrections:

The great difficulty in education is to get experience out of ideas.
– George Santayana

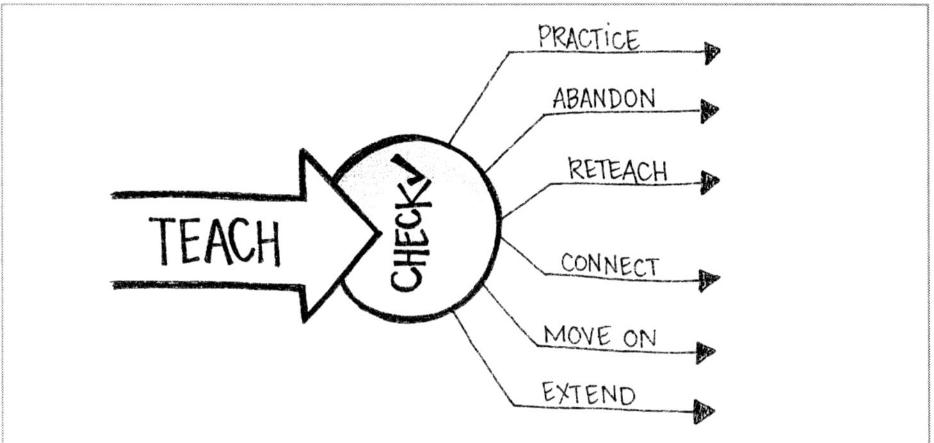

Practice. When students are at the cusp of (upon or near) mastery, it is an effective move to provide additional opportunities for practice and rehearsal of newly acquired skills. This early practice can consolidate gains and prevent regression from mastery (Landauer & Bjork, 1978).

Re-teach. Sometimes it actually saves time to just start over. If, upon assessment, a significant number of students are a significant distance from mastery, then a new approach may be in order. The teacher should "own" the change. "Friends, the way I just taught that did not make much sense to many of you. Give me another chance, OK? Let's try it this way." The new way, of course, should be quite different from the first way with new activities, new groupings, new sequences, new examples, and, hopefully, new results.

Abandon. Well, temporarily abandon, anyway. Sometimes, the best way to success is to delay. Perhaps it is too late in the afternoon to begin a new concept, or a fire drill interrupts the class's focus, or a discipline issue stirs up too much anxiety. In cases such as this, a smart decision may be to delay the lesson until a time when success is more likely. Kenny Rogers had the right idea in his hit country song, "The Gambler." Rogers sang *"...You've got to know when to hold 'em and know when to fold 'em..."* (Rogers, 1978).

A man paints with his brains and not with his hands.

- Michelangelo

Education is all a matter of building bridges.
- Ralph Ellison

Move on. Sometimes, assessment shows that students are ahead of the expected pace. In this case, practice repetitions can be reduced, time can be saved, and the next concept or skill can be introduced sooner than planned.

Extend. State and national standards are written as minimums, not maximums. Sometimes, as students master a concept, the teacher might decide to teach it to a higher level, or deepen students' understanding beyond what is expected.

Connect. Sometimes, even when students have done well enough in mastering an isolated skill or concept, the teacher may decide to spend time building connections to other content, other experiences, or other skills. Knowing that elaboration promotes transfer (Caine & Caine, 1994), the teacher might intentionally spend time building or connecting schema for the purpose of future recall and transfer (see also chapter 9, Connection).

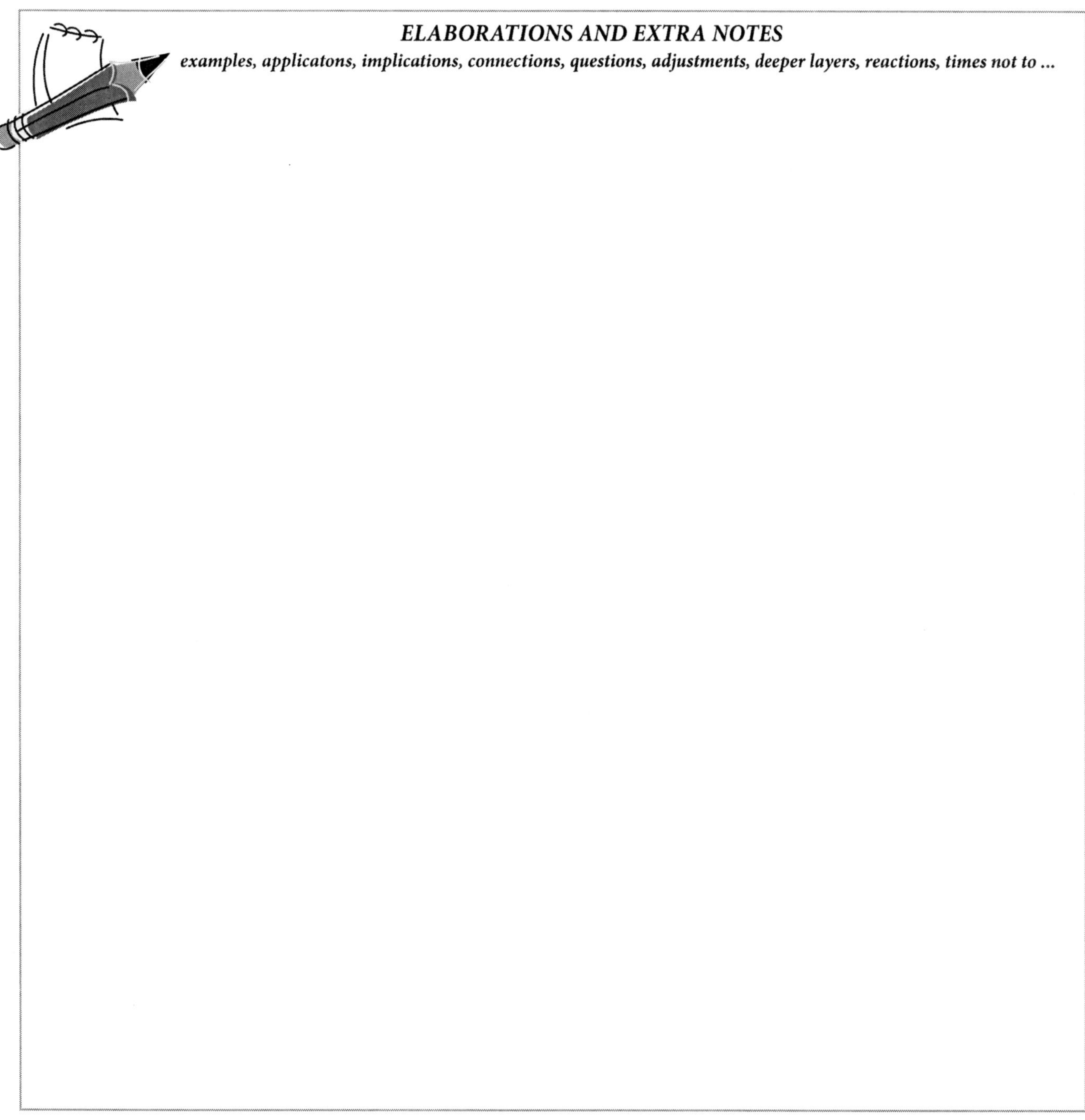

ELABORATIONS AND EXTRA NOTES

examples, applicatons, implications, connections, questions, adjustments, deeper layers, reactions, times not to ...

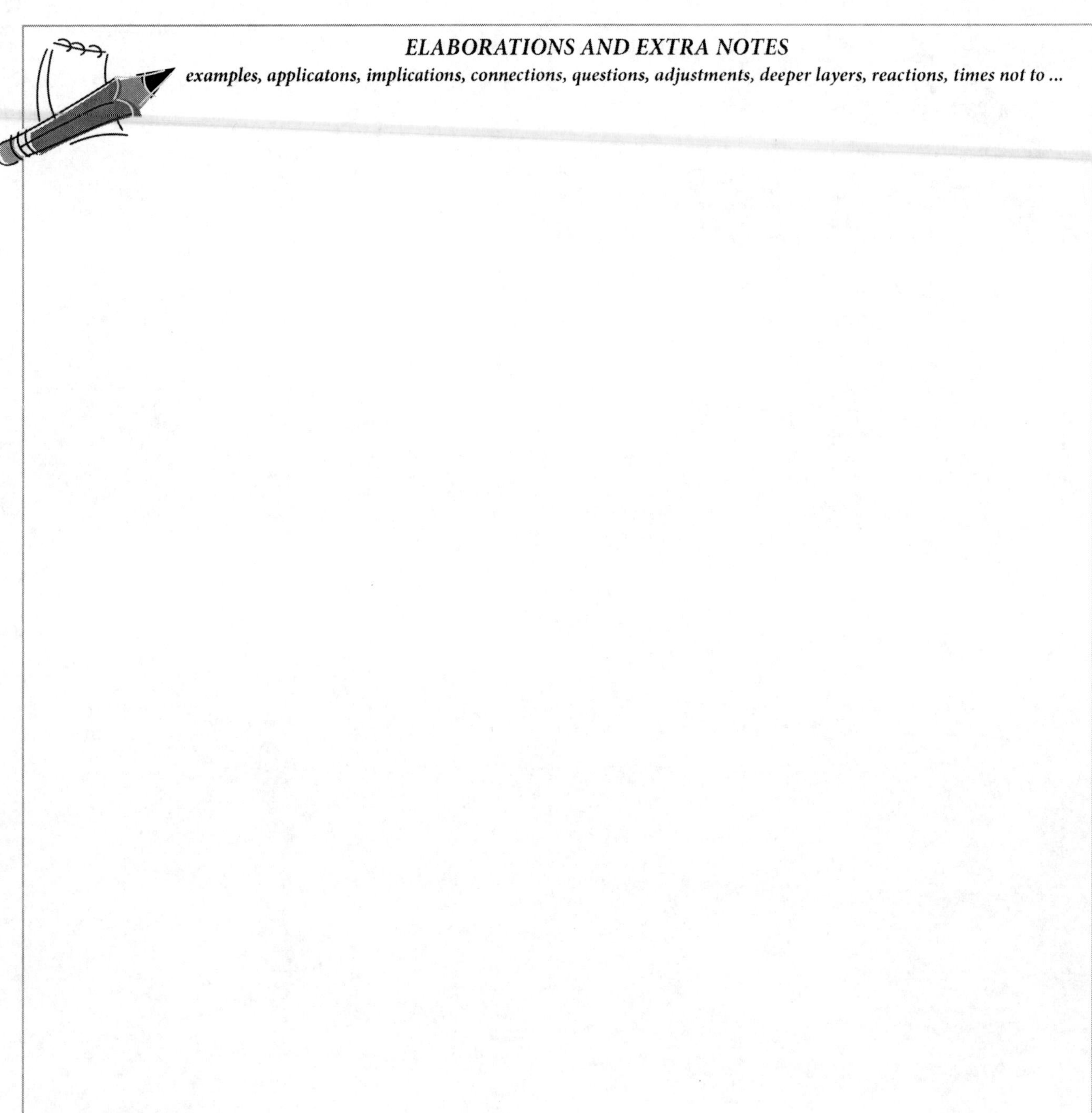
ELABORATIONS AND EXTRA NOTES
examples, applicatons, implications, connections, questions, adjustments, deeper layers, reactions, times not to ...

THEME 7

CONSCIOUS ATTENTION

FIELD NOTES:

Conscious Attention

Definition. The ability of the teacher to gain students' attention, focus it on relevant learning tasks, and avoid distractions.

Elaboration. From the beginning of time, it seems, teachers have been imploring their students to "pay attention." And for good reason, attention is not the same as learning, but it is a prerequisite to learning. We tend to actually learn, (remember) a small percentage of all the things to which we pay some attention (Sylwester & Choo, 1992). Therefore, a teacher's ability to gain, focus, direct, and deepen student attention is essential to classroom success. The absence of student attention is doubly detrimental in that even well designed lessons involving rich learning experiences are only partially effective in the absence of students' full attention and engagement.

Information processing theory suggests that the human brain handles incoming information like a computer would (Orey, 2001). Diagrams such as Figure 1, (see next page), are often used to depict how the informational processing model works (Rutherford, 1995).

What sculpture is to a block of marble, education is to the soul.

– Joseph Addison

FIGURE 1

The Information Processing Model

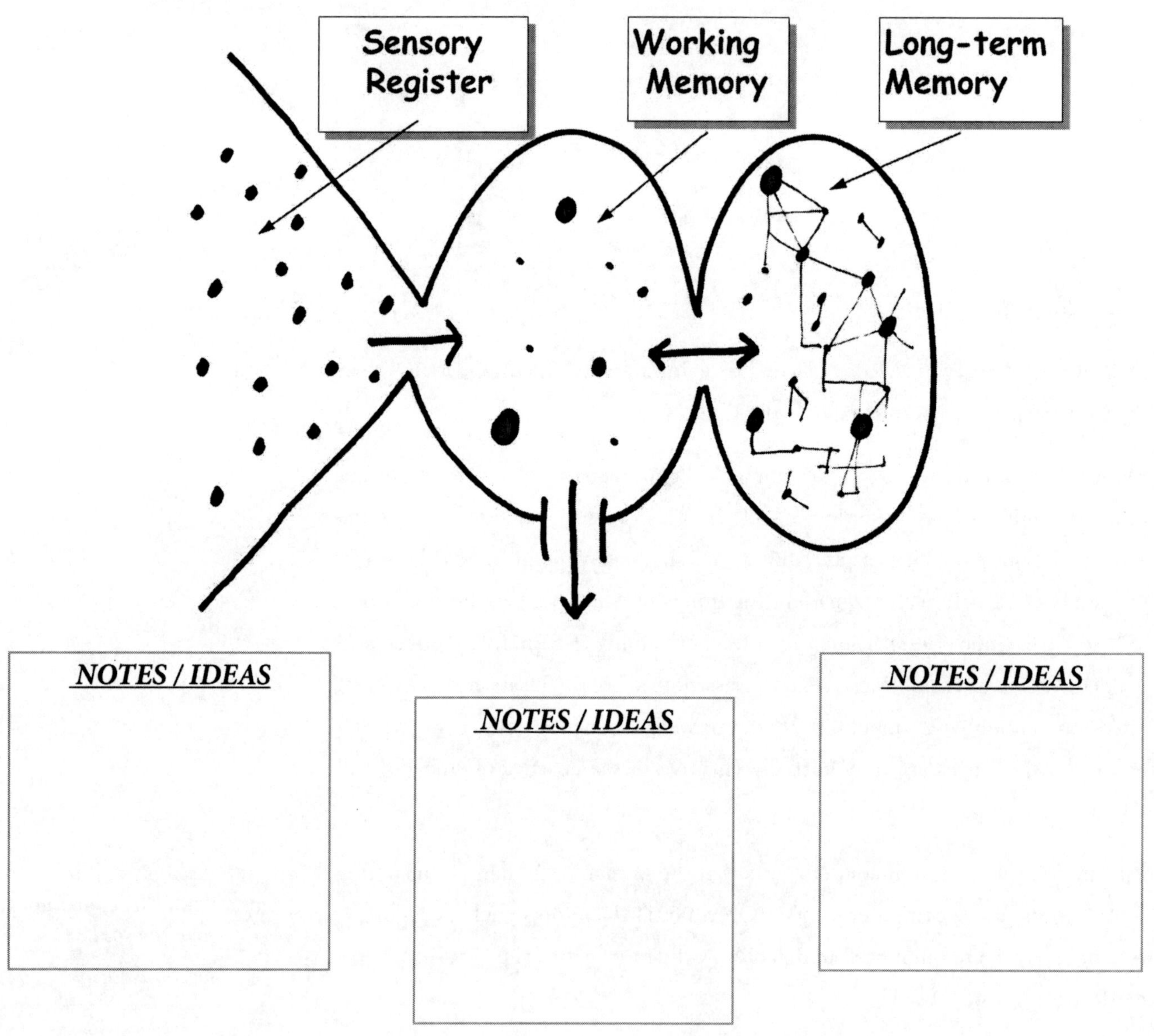

NOTES / IDEAS

NOTES / IDEAS

NOTES / IDEAS

Discreet chunks (Miller, 1956) of information, such as numbers, words, faces, songs, or ideas are represented by dots in the diagram. The chunks move first from the environment into the sensory register where they are scanned for importance. A few chunks, those deemed to be most important, move into the working memory (also called short-term memory) for closer consideration, and then some chunks, because of rehearsal or inherent relevance, are moved to long-term memory for storage and recall (Caine & Caine, 1994). Attention, according to the information processing model, can be thought of as the brain's extraction of a few important chunks from the sensory register. The chunks that are selected can be said to receive our *conscious attention.* Those that are not selected pass through our subconscious, but never occupy a place in consciousness, or working memory.

A radio receiver operates much the same way and can be a helpful analogy. At any moment a radio receives signals from many stations, but "tunes in" only one and excludes the others. This "tuning in" function is what allows the human brain to receive many signals , but "pay attention" to only one. In the classroom, teachers can help students "tune in" their focus on a learning task and exclude other attentions.

At any moment a radio receives signals from many stations, but "tunes in" only one and excludes the others.

The artist is a receptacle for emotions that come from all over the place: from the sky, from the earth, from a scrap of paper, from a passing shape, from a spider's web.

– Pablo Picasso

Three ways to gain and direct student attention.

Invitation. Humans can direct their conscious attention. Our attention is under our intentional control. We don't always direct our attention by conscious choice, and we often do not, but, we can direct our attention when we choose to do so. Therefore, one simple, but effective, way to engage student's attention is to *invite* them to intentionally extract a specific chunk from the sensory register. A teacher might say "I'd like you to pay special attention to the next step in the experiment. Something surprising is about to happen and I don't want you to miss it." Many students, if not all, will accept the teacher's invitation and intentionally direct their conscious attention to the experiment. The key to a successful invitation is to cause the student to make a *conscious* choice concerning his immediate attention. If left to subconscious processing, the student's brain might choose to focus on any number of targets. A teacher once said "Touch your left ear if you're paying attention and your right ear if you are not." In order to comply, each student had to stop and consciously consider whether or not he was paying attention… and in so doing, he was, by design, then paying attention.

Discrepancy. As a feature of our survival instincts, we are compelled to pay attention, if only for a moment, to anything that is different, surprising, or discrepant. In a sea of vehicles on the freeway, the bright yellow/orange school bus stands out. Many states require that hunters wear blaze orange so as not to be mistaken for game as they move through the forest. A quick glance at the breaker box is sufficient to tell which breaker is tripped. The principle of discrepancy is at work in each of these examples. The brain is designed to closely examine anything that doesn't fit into the expected background.

Teachers can use the brain's innate recognition of discrepant events to direct student attention. A teacher who usually talks fast, but slows to a crawl for effect, enjoys a brief burst of attention from students who recognize the change in pace as a discrepancy. Standing in a new place, using a different color marker, speaking in an unusual accent, or asking students to stand and face east, can all invoke an attention response due to the discrepancy of the action.

A process that opposes the attention enhancing properties of discrepancy is *habituation*. Habituation is the brain's ability and tendency to withhold conscious attention from any stimuli that is regularly repeated. Upon entering a room for a meeting, one might notice an annoying hum in the ventilation system. After thirty minutes of the meeting, however, the hum is barely noticed. Due to habituation, some people don't mind living near an airport or railroad tracks, since the loud noises are no longer discrepant, but a part of the expected environment. Where classroom attention is concerned, discrepancy can be a powerful ally. Habituation, however, is the enemy of conscious attention.

Two cautions need to be considered when using discrepancy. First, don't overuse discrepancy. If repeated too often or too regularly an event ceases to be discrepant. I suppose the first time a teacher ever flipped the lights on and off in a classroom, students stopped what they were doing and paid attention. If used too often though, the effect is habituation, not discrepancy. "That's just the way the lights work in this classroom," a student thinks to himself as they start blinking on and off again.

Second, don't make things too discrepant. The discrepancy, if too vivid, can become the object of memory rather than the intended curriculum. I recall Dr. Madeline Hunter once saying "Don't use a live elephant to teach the color gray." Well said.

Emotional Hook. We tend to focus first and best on events that have some emotional significance. Perhaps as an expression of our survival tendencies, we tend to focus our attention on things that trigger an emotional or affective

He who studies books alone will know how things ought to be, and he who studies men will know how they are.

- Charles Caleb Colton

The mediator of the inexpressible is the work of art.

– Johann Wolfgang von Goethe

response. Events or items that evoke anger, sympathy, curiosity, affection, jealousy, or intrigue command our attention to a greater degree than events or items than conjure a less affective response (Pekrun, 1992). This is not to suggest that teachers should whip their students into an emotional frenzy for the sake of a little extra attention. Subtle emotional cues such as eye contact, facial expressions, proximity, curiosity, challenge, irony, or humor can be all that's needed to shepherd a chunk from a student's sensory register into a student's *conscious attention*.

Final thoughts on conscious attention. Using the strategies of invitation, discrepancy, and emotional hook, a teacher *can* command students' conscious attention at any time. This does not suggest, however, that a teacher *should* seek students' focused attention throughout the school day. In fact, that would be impossible. Much of the struggle that some teachers seem to have with student attention springs from an expectation that they should obtain it and keep it throughout much or all of the instructional day. A more successful approach seeks a balance among at least three types of student attention (Rutherford, 2001).

Focused attention. Using invitation, discrepancy, and emotional hook, a teacher can seek all students' focused attention on a specific event or task. It is difficult to sustain this kind of focused attention so teachers do well to seek it in short spurts and at choice times throughout the day.

Dispersed attention. It is natural for students to pay attention to various learning tasks and events as directed by their own interests and choices. This type of attention can be sustained for longer periods of time. All students are attending, but to different targets and in different ways.

Inward attention. Students should also have ample opportunities to turn their attention inward through reflection, meta-cognition, self-awareness, and individual preparation or closure.

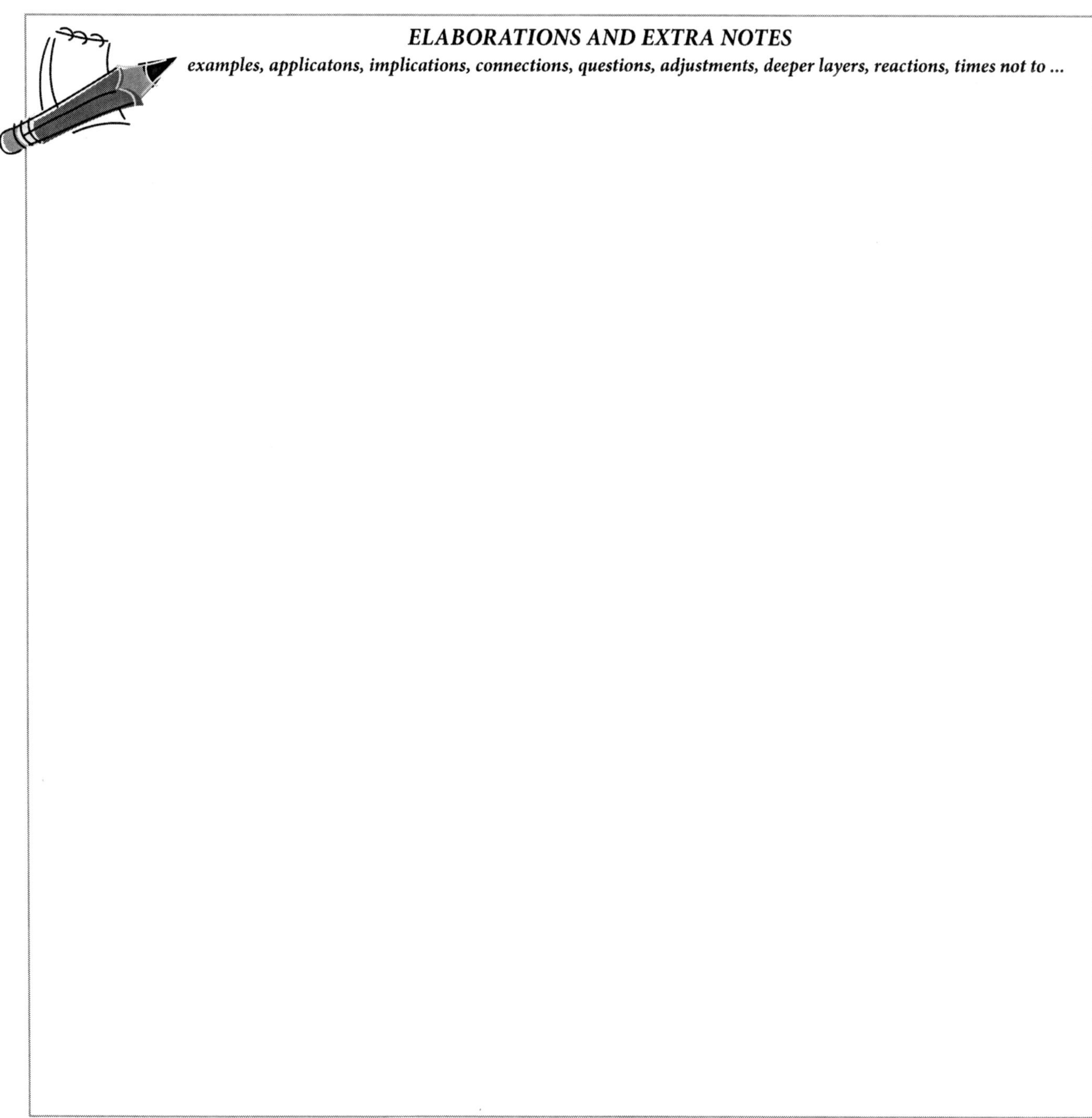

ELABORATIONS AND EXTRA NOTES

examples, applicatons, implications, connections, questions, adjustments, deeper layers, reactions, times not to ...

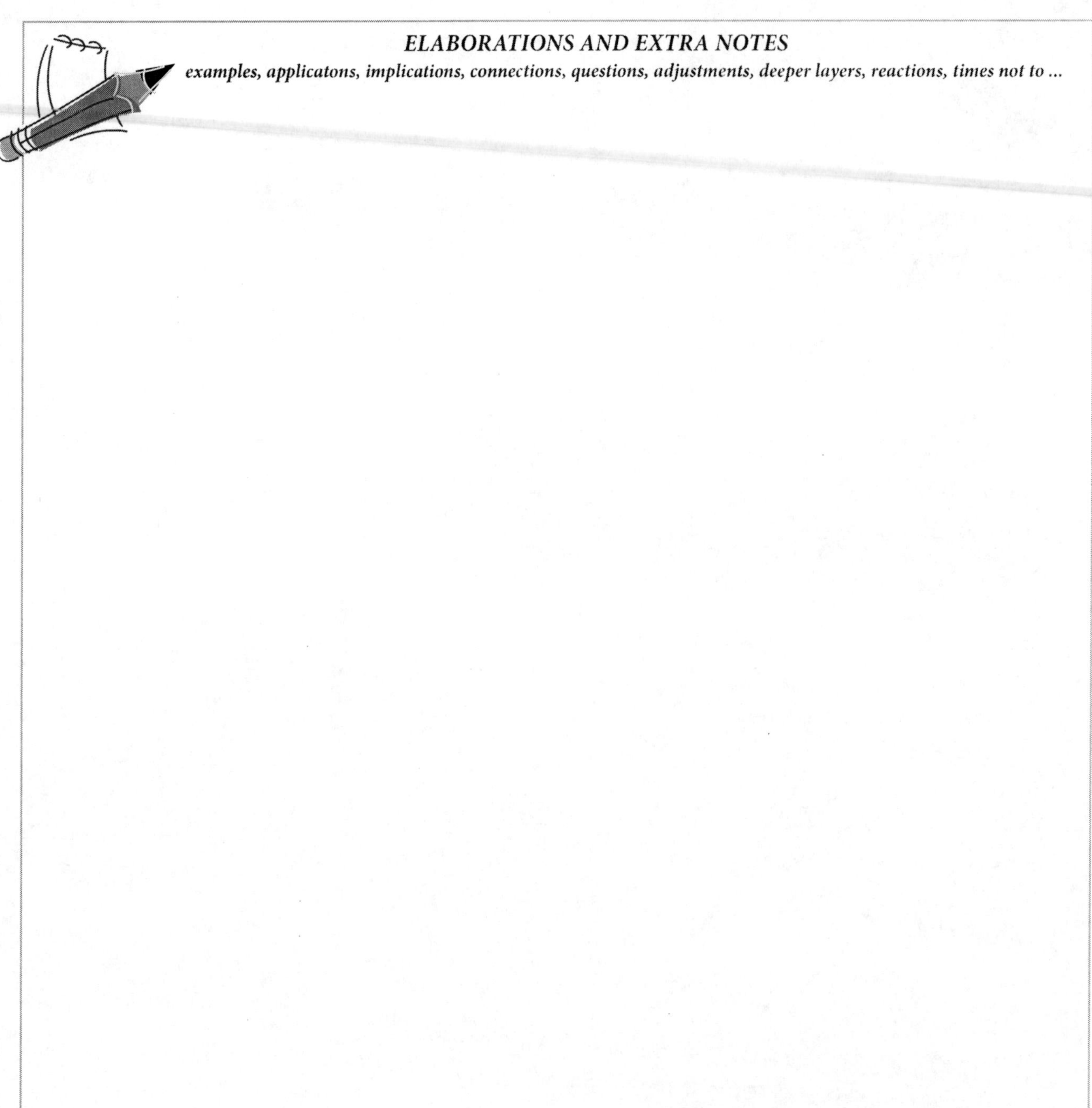
ELABORATIONS AND EXTRA NOTES
examples, applicatons, implications, connections, questions, adjustments, deeper layers, reactions, times not to ...

THEME 8
CHUNKING

FIELD NOTES:

Chunking

Definition. The ability of the teacher to segment the curriculum and learning activities into manageable portions to avoid overwhelming students' capacity for new information.

Elaboration. According to information processing theory, we have a limited capacity to consciously handle incoming information (Cowan, 1997). Rather than being able to attend to an unlimited number of items simultaneously, we can attend to only a few. While this might seem like an unfortunate design flaw in human memory, it is actually necessary to give us our powers of focus and attention. Adults have a larger capacity than children, but it is still limited (Miller, 1956). Our capacity to consider incoming information is limited to a handful of chunks. A chunk can be thought of as a discrete "package" of information. Chunks can be small like the number 5 or large, like a telephone number- 704-825-8562. Chunks can be simple like the definition of "previous", or complex, like how to drive a car from a stop sign up an icy hill with a manual transmission. Whether our chunks are large or small, simple or complex, we seem to have only about

It is a bit like a good juggler can keep several balls in the air while holding onto only one at a time.

seven of them available to us at any given moment (Miller, 1956; Simon, 1974). Chunking, then, is the process of combining small chunks into larger ones and building the complexity and sophistication of chunks to increase the quantity and quality of learning.

A working memory overload (WMO) is a state of rapid forgetting induced by a task that exceeds the capacity of working memory. As teachers seek to avoid WMOs for their students, they do well to remember the two limiting factors of working memory.

Working memory has a limited capacity. Adults have a working memory capacity of approximately seven discrete chunks (Miller, 1956). Since we hardly ever seek to concentrate on completely discreet chunks simultaneously, it is more helpful to consider that adults can manage three or four representations, or collections of discreet chucks at once (Cowen, 1997). Children have a smaller capacity (Ross-Sheehy, Oakes, & Luck, 2003), perhaps managing one or two representations, rather than three or four for adults (Barner, Thalwitz, Wood, Yang, & Carey, 2007; Moher, Tuerk, & Feigenson, 2012).

Learning is a result of listening, which in turn leads to even better listening and attentiveness to the other person. In other words, to learn from the child, we must have empathy, and empathy grows as we learn.

– Alice Miller

Keeping this limitation in mind, teachers would do well to keep new information demands at or below the working memory capacity of their students. For example, a first grade teacher knows not to give multiple step directions to students. This would exceed capacity and lead to an overload.

It is important to help students to combine and consolidate information. For example, through several rounds of practice, a teacher could help students see the four steps in long division as one process, rather than four discrete steps. This process of increasing the size and complexity of chunks is what allows students, even young ones with limited working memory capacity, to build rich understandings and meaningful connections among disparate pieces of information.

Working memory functions as a serial (one at a time) processor. A student's working memory can attend to only one task at a time. Humans can switch back and forth between tasks rapidly, appearing to be multi-tasking, but at any given split second, they are handling just one mental task at a time (Sternberg, 1966). Again, this is not so much a limitation on our ability to multi-task, as it is a valuable ability to focus and concentrate on individual tasks.

The fact that humans can only focus on one task at a time doesn't mean we can't have several things in our sphere of attention simultaneously. We must choose, however, which item will be in the foreground, as we relegate all other attentions to the background (Townsend & Fific, 2004). It is a bit like a good juggler can keep several balls in the air while holding onto only one a time. As I am writing this chapter, I'm also waiting for the delivery truck to deliver a package, keeping an eye on our 5 month old puppy, Wilson, and copying some video files from this computer to another. Writing is in the foreground and the rest is in the background. That is, until Wilson barks or I see the delivery truck pull into the driveway. Then, the foreground and background trade places, if just for a moment.

It is only as we develop others that we permanently succeed.
– Harvey S. Firestone

All real education is the architecture of the soul.
– William Bennett

The juggler grabs another ball and the one he was holding is now in the air.

As teachers understand this process and its subtleties, they are more capable of orchestrating a classroom environment that limits giving students multiple foreground tasks simultaneously. It is difficult for students to listen *and* take notes, to finish their homework *and* listen to the afternoon announcements, or to follow along as text is read aloud *and* spot descriptive words.

Students also benefit when their teachers appreciate some of the nuance of foreground/background attention. Some of the most productive classrooms have multiple processes going on at the same time; group work, individual work, soft music playing, teachers holding conversations with individual students, centers, clean-up, and so on. The trick is to help students keep the foreground in focus and not let the background steal the show too often.

An understanding of serial processing can also benefit behavior management. Rather than asking students to not do something or to stop doing something, ask them to do something else. The brain can't focus on both so the new behavior displaces the old one. Instead of saying "Thomas, please stop talking." A teacher might say "Thomas, will you use your left pinkie finger to point to the picture of the elephant on page 45?" If Thomas complies, he must, at least temporarily, stop talking.

Because of serial processing it is difficult for us to *not* do something. Have you ever tried to not smile, or not giggle in church, or not touch a button? If you're a golfer you know how hard it is to *not* hit it in the pond. Our youngest son, Bennett, was a serial milk spiller as a toddler. I remember it didn't help much to say "Bennett, don't spill your milk." It was more effective to say "Bennett, hold on with both hands." So we humans can't focus on many things at once, but we also can't focus on nothing.

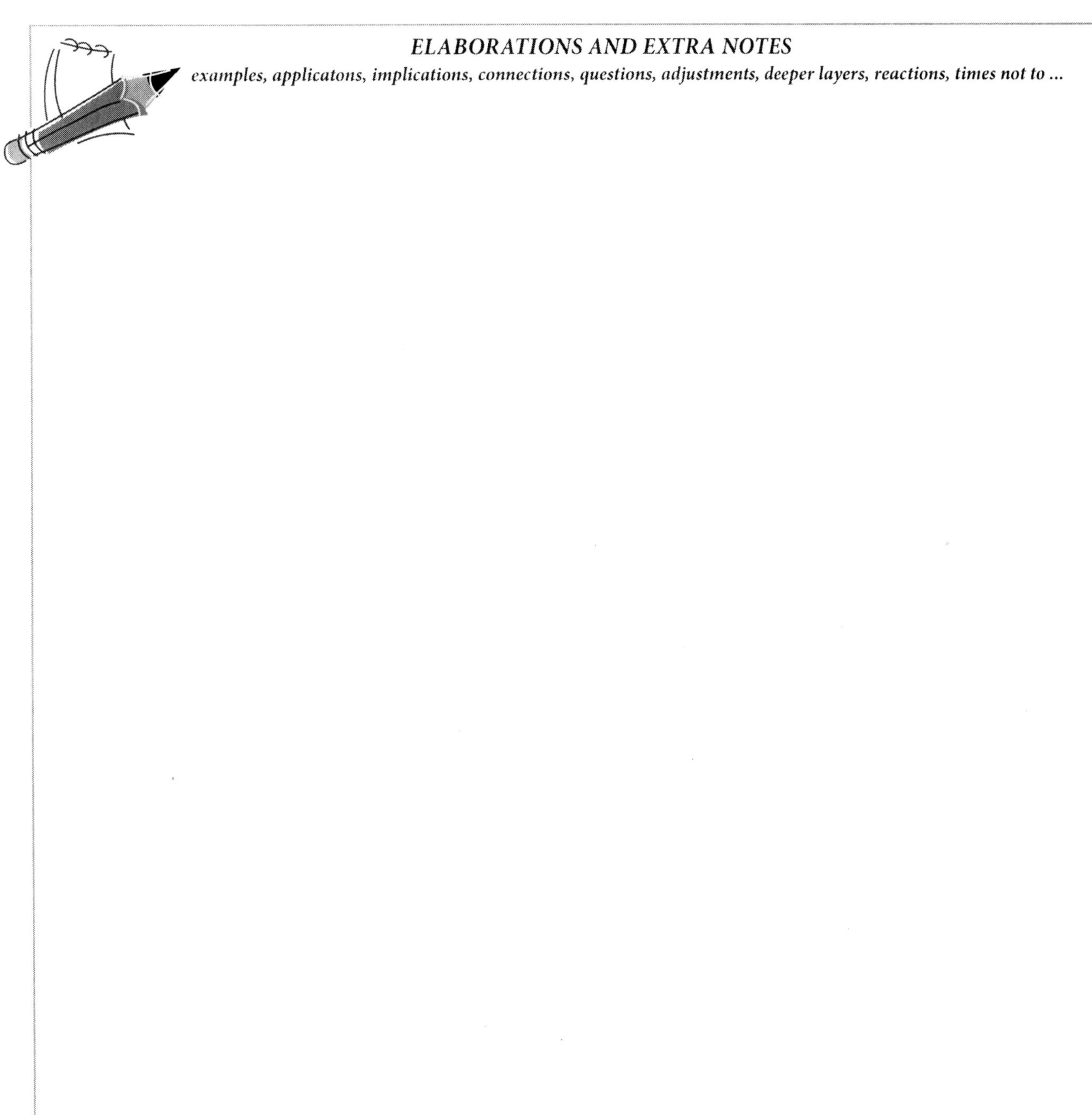

ELABORATIONS AND EXTRA NOTES
examples, applicatons, implications, connections, questions, adjustments, deeper layers, reactions, times not to ...

ELABORATIONS AND EXTRA NOTES
examples, applicatons, implications, connections, questions, adjustments, deeper layers, reactions, times not to ...

THEME **9**

CONNECTION

Connection

Definition. The ability of the teacher to establish a mental link between the intended learning and past learning or experiences.

Elaboration. Of all the twenty-three themes, Connection is perhaps the single theme that is most directly aimed at how the human brain naturally learns (Bartlett, 1932). We know that as we learn, the brain is constantly seeking to connect things, to look for patterns, to see similarities, and to form familiar categories (Caine & Caine, 1994). Whenever we encounter something new, it is natural for us to think of past knowledge or experience that is similar (Tse, Langston, Kakeyama, Bethus, Spooner, Wood, Witter, & Morris, 2007). As we describe a new food to a friend, we might say "it tastes like chicken." To describe a new puppy, we might say "he looks like a cross between a poodle and a beagle." If someone is giving us directions, they might say "it's a half mile past that big red barn on the right." In all these examples, we are building on what the brain already knows or has experienced. Since we know what chicken tastes like, what poodles look like, and where the red barn is, we can build on our past knowledge and experience to quickly and effectively learn new things.

To the extent that we are all educated and informed, we will be more equipped to deal with the gut issues that tend to divide us.

- Caroline Kennedy

Teachers who recognize this natural process, and capitalize on it, are teaching in a way that is congruent to the brain's innate tendencies (Nummela and Rosengren, 1986). The social studies teacher who suggests that the three branches of the federal government operate a lot like the game paper-rock scissors is using connection. The science teacher who explains to 9th graders that molecules in the liquid phase move just like students in a crowded hallway during a class change is using connection. In the 1984 movie *The Karate Kid*, Mr. Miyagi used connection when he taught Daniel to wax his car. Remember "wax on (clockwise rotation) – wax off (counterclockwise)". Mr. Myagi used those movements as a connection the next day when he taught Daniel how to block incoming punches from the right (wax on) and from the left (wax off).

Connection is a powerful tool, but it is wise to remember that it can work both for and against learning (Rosenfeld, 1988). When the learner connects new information to prior knowledge or experience and the connection enhances the learning of the new material, then connection's effect is positive toward the intended learning. But when the learner connects new information to prior knowledge or experience that does not produce the intended learning, then the connection's effect is negative (Nummela and Rosengren, 1986). We might call this a missed connection or a misconception.

The art of art, the glory of expression and the sunshine of the light of letters, is simplicity.
– Walt Whitman

Many students have a misconception about what causes the Earth's seasons. Remembering past experiences with fire, they recall that it is warmer close to the fire and colder farther away. They then mistakenly connect that relationship to their understanding of the Earth's seasons, believing that summer is when the Earth is closer to the sun and winter is when the Earth is farther away. The truth is that seasons are caused by the Earth's 23.5° degree tilt on its axis. As the Earth revolves around the Sun the northern hemisphere tilts toward the sun in the summer and away in the winter. It's this tilting toward and away from the sun that causes the seasons, not the distance from the sun.

Some common causes of misconceptions.

Lack of processing time. When students are asked to learn much new material in a short time, with few opportunities for processing, the tendency is to make the *first* available connection, rather than to think through the possibilities and make the *best* available connection. If a person is asked to repeat the word "white" ten times and then is quickly asked the question "What do cows drink? They will often respond "milk." That's not the best answer, but it is the next and fastest connection among the terms white, cow, and drink. If we were to try that activity and add the command "think about it for 10 seconds before you reply," most people would then answer, "Cows drink water." The extra processing time gave the brain a chance to move beyond the first possible connection and select a better alternative.

Oversimplification. To teach is to simplify. Great teachers can take very complex content and make it accessible, even to beginning learners. But taken too far, simplification can lead to misconception. Photosynthesis is a complex chemical process. To simplify it, a teacher might say "Photosynthesis is the process by which plants eat food for energy." That's a tempting connection. Students know how humans eat food and know how digestion works to turn food into energy.

Some students believe that Hawaii is about forty-five miles southwest of San Diego, CA.

It has been said that 80% of what people learn is visual.
- Allen Klein

But, it's an oversimplification. Plants don't eat, chew, swallow, digest, or excrete. Using the terms "food" and "eat" will likely get in the way of learning the real chemical process of photosynthesis.

Teaching in two dimensions. If a learner's first experience with a three-dimensional reality is a two-dimensional representation of that reality, the possibility for misconception is greater (Goldberg & McDermott, 1987). Many students learn about the moon's phases from a textbook with pictures (2-D) of a full, half, quarter, and crescent moon. This can lead to all sorts of explanations of the moon's phases. A teacher does better to hang a volleyball from the ceiling, turn off the lights, and use a flashlight (standing in for the sun) to show how half the moon is always light and half is always dark. Then by moving around the moon (the volleyball) they can see that phases are due to their location as they look at the half light/half dark moon.

Some students believe that Hawaii is located about 45 miles southwest of San Diego, CA. That's where the 2-D map places it to save space. If the student learned the location of Hawaii from a globe, the misconception would be unlikely. It is important that initial experiences with three dimensional reality be in three dimensions.

Tips or making connections and avoiding misconceptions.

The connection must first exist in the mind of the learner. If there is any doubt about this, it is a good idea for the teacher to first provide the knowledge/experience to be connected to and *then* execute the connection.

The connection should be made actively. Each individual student should engage in the connection, not just watch as other students participate. Classroom demonstrations, where one person does something and the rest observe, can be useful, but are not the best strategy for making and remembering connections.

Watch for, and test for, misconceptions. Since connection is an invisible process, the teacher can only hope that the right links are being made. It is best to assume that there will be misconceptions and to predict where they are most likely to occur. When the likelihood of a misconception is high, consider adding processing time, check for oversimplification, and be sure to teach three dimensional content in three dimensions.

A good teacher is a determined person.

– Gilbert Highet

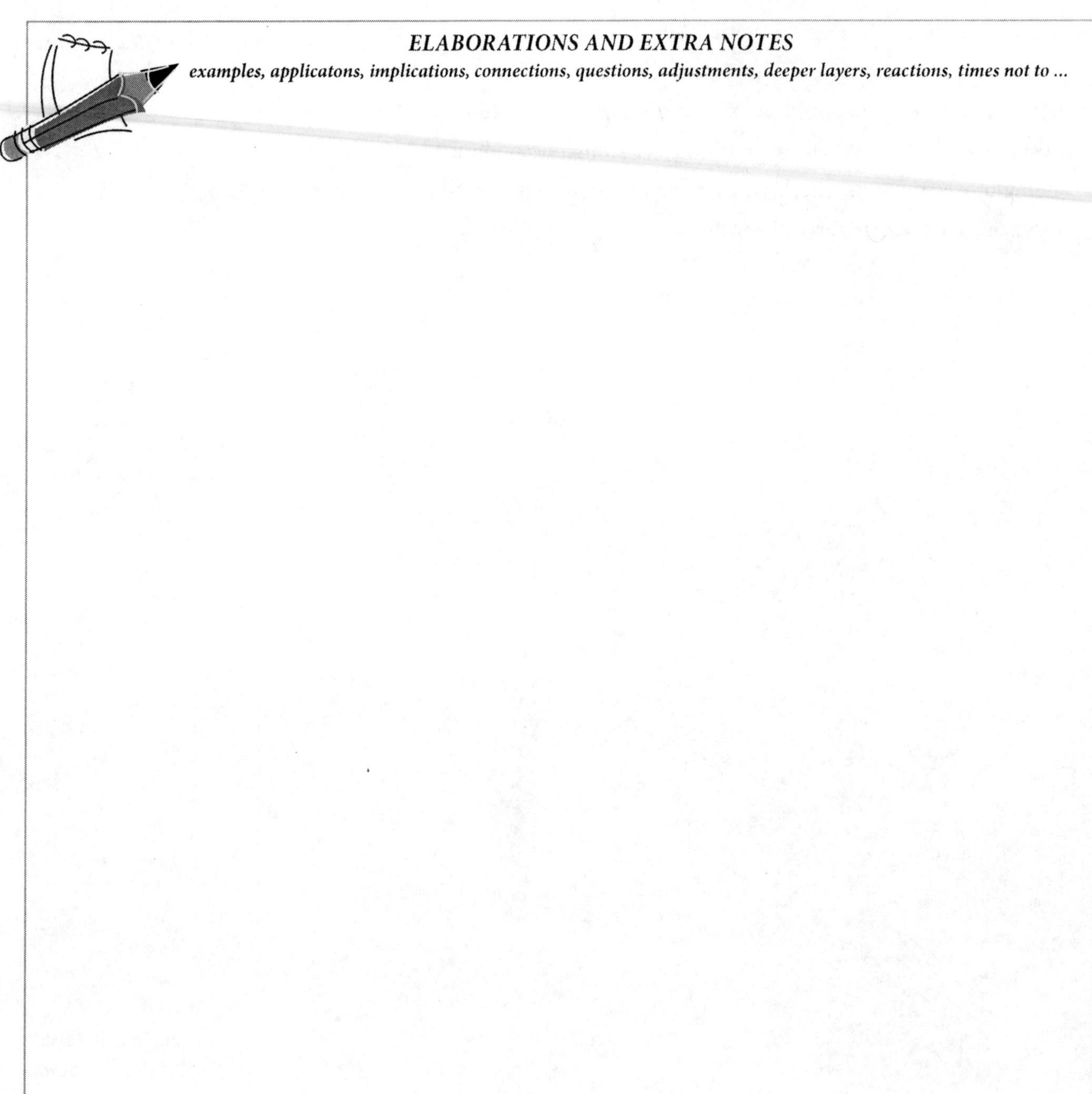
ELABORATIONS AND EXTRA NOTES
examples, applicatons, implications, connections, questions, adjustments, deeper layers, reactions, times not to ...

THEME 10
PRACTICE

FIELD NOTES:

How do you get to Carnegie Hall?... Practice, practice, practice.

Practice

Definition. The ability of the teacher to improve recall and application of learning through effective rehearsal, repeated effort, drill, repetition, study, and review.

Elaboration. The famous joke goes, "How do you get to Carnegie Hall?" The punch line, "Practice. Practice. Practice." Practice has long been recognized as an essential element in learning. In reflecting on thousands of classroom observations, I would say, as a rough estimate, that 50% of all classroom time is devoted to practicing things. Great teaching is not simply the presentation of new material in an interesting, relevant manner. It involves designing quality experiences for students such that, as they engage in the experiences, they work out their mastery of the curriculum (Schlechty, 2011). An important part of the design for this "working out" of students' mastery is the design for quality practice. Call it repetition, drill, rehearsal, review, study, or practice. By any name, a key effect of practice is that knowledge and skills become established in long term memory so that recall and application can occur in the future (Atkinson and Shifflin, 1971).

Based on numerous observations of classroom instruction, interviews with coaches, band directors, drama teachers, and others who routinely design practice sessions, and a thorough scan of the literature on the topic, here are some success principles that can serve as a guide to designing and facilitating productive practice.

Success principles for practice.

Keep practice sessions short so focus and intensity can remain high. The key to productive practice is focus, intention, motivation, and intensity (Ericsson, 2007), not just the amount of practice or the length of time one practices. Long sessions of mindless, low intensity practice can even serve to reduce recall and application (Hunter, 1982).

A lesson can be learned from watching the practice of elite athletes and musicians. To reach their high level of performance they must accumulate many, many hours of practice. Their daily routine, however, finds them practicing for many short, intense spurts distributed across time. K. Anders Ericsson (2007), in his study of elite performers found that expert violinists, for example, accumulated

The function of education is to teach one to think intensively and to think critically. Intelligence plus character - that is the goal of true education.

– Martin Luther King, Jr.

over 10,000 hours of deliberate practice to reach virtuoso status. Deliberate practice, according to Ericsson, is exhausting and intense and therefore cannot be performed for long periods of time.

Practice small chunks, then, move to larger combinations. Human short term memory has a limited capacity (Miller, 1956) and practice sessions are more productive when the amount of material to be practiced is limited. Once recall of the smaller chunks is achieved, they can be combined to form more elaborate organizations. (Atkinson and Shiffrin, 1971; Hunter, 1982). For example, an organist might practice the left hand in a piece, then the right hand, then the foot pedals, then put the parts together to form the entire performance.

Attend to energy and motivation needs during practice. Practice requires energy. Focused, intense practice requires even more energy. Energy can be increased by introducing games, goals, incentives, encouragement and feedback (Ericsson, 2009).

Provide knowledgeable feedback during practice. Practice sessions are most productive when students are provided abundant, immediate, and specific feedback on their work (Hattie & Timperley, 2007). High quality feedback encourages students to persist in the practice activities.

Move quickly to elaborative practice. It is easier to remember items if we know more about them, beyond their definition, spelling, or representation. The more students can make connections among ideas and concepts and associate them with other items from prior learning and experience, the more likely they are to be remembered and applied (Raaijmakers and Shifflin, 1981) (Smith, 1979).

Conduct practice in the visual, spatial, and cognitive domains. Recall is enhanced when students are asked to engage using both internal (cognitive) and external (visual and spatial) processing methodologies (Tigner, 1999). The

Art is not a study of positive reality, it is the seeking for ideal truth.
– John Ruskin

regions of the brain that process and remember images and spatial relationships are well developed in humans and can be important aids for remembering more cognitive or abstract items (Awh, Jonides & Reuter-Lorenz, 1998).

Distribute practice sessions across time. Recall is enhanced when the brain has an opportunity to consolidate memories before adding new ones. Also, the periodic revisiting of a memory strengthens it and increases the ability to recall it in the future. Therefore, cramming for an exam is much less productive than reviewing for it over a period of days or weeks (Baddeley, 1986).

Design the difficulty of the practice to be challenging, but attainable. Motivation to engage in practice is weak if the task to be practiced is viewed as too easy or too hard. Motivation is strongest when the task is viewed as challenging, but within the capabilities of the student. Optimally, the task difficulty of the practice increases in step with skill development, maintaining the learner in the zone where challenge and ability overlap (Vygotsky, 1978).

Don't let schooling interfere with your education.

– Mark Twain

ELABORATIONS AND EXTRA NOTES

examples, applicatons, implications, connections, questions, adjustments, deeper layers, reactions, times not to ...

ELABORATIONS AND EXTRA NOTES
examples, applicatons, implications, connections, questions, adjustments, deeper layers, reactions, times not to ...

THEME **11**

Personal Relevance

Personal Relevance

Definition. The ability of the teacher to embed the intended curriculum into issues and contexts that are linked to students' personal lives, survival instincts, or immediate well-being.

Elaboration. Students engage deeply and learn quickly when the curriculum is embedded in issues and contexts that students see as linked to themselves (Sylwester, 1995; Wolfe, 2010). This enhanced engagement and learning is further strengthened if the link is to the students' survival instincts or immediate wellbeing (Damasio, 1994). Human beings, it seems, are particularly interested in themselves and especially in their own survival and immediate well-being. Teachers can use this feature of human nature to their advantage (Wolfe, 2010). After watching many teachers, who are naturally gifted at this, work with students, I think I've figured out how they do it. Here's how it seems to work. First, they select an issue or context that is personally relevant to students. Then, they use it as a "container" to hold the intended curriculum. The trick is to get students' brains to see and engage with the container (something personally relevant) and, in so doing, to also engage with the contents of the container, the curriculum.

It is a miracle that curiosity survives formal education.
– Albert Einstein

Every production of an artist should be the expression of an adventure of his soul.
- W. Somerset Maugham

We have an old dog at our house. His name is Berkley. Berkley does not like to take pills. I've tried to reason with Berkley about taking the pills. It does not seem to matter to him that the pills are good for him and that if he takes them, he will feel better. Berkley's favorite food is cheese. He absolutely loves it and his tail starts wagging the second he believes there may be some cheese in his near future. So, to get him to take the pills, I have to use the cheese as a "container." He wolfs down the cheese, and in so doing, gets the benefit of the pills.

Talented teachers operate similarly. Instead of reasoning with students that they should pay attention to the curriculum because it will benefit them in the future, they find some "cheese," wrap the intended content into the cheese, and then watch the students gobble it all down.

A kindergarten teacher begins letter formation with the letters contained in students' first names, not in ABC order. Students work hard and long on forming these "special" letters.

A middle school art teacher teaches "proportionality" by printing an image of each student's face on graph paper. He then asks students to sketch an enlarged image onto another sheet of blank graph paper. No one makes a peep as the students focus on recreating their own faces.

A 9th grade English teacher asks students to translate passages of Shakespeare's *Romeo and Juliet* from Elizabethan language into "Tweets" of 140 or fewer characters. As they translate, the students become engrossed in the true meaning of Shakespeare's words so they can accurately recreate the sentiments in Twitter language.

A high school biology teacher introduces basic genetics by asking students to create a personal genetic profile including eye color, closed or open ear folds, widow's peak vs. straight hairlines, and length of index vs. ring fingers. Students are riveted on the lesson as they learn more and more about themselves and their inherited traits.

In each case, the teacher employed a similar approach. Instead of simply teaching the content directly, the teacher first selected a personally relevant "container" for the content. Then, the teacher carefully selected the content that would be a particularly good fit for the container. The sequence of the process is important. Choosing the personally relevant container comes first, not the selection of the content.

So, using personal relevance is not so much asking oneself, "How can I make this content personally relevant?" It is, rather, asking oneself, "What is already personally relevant?" And then, once that question has been answered, asking "What content is a particularly good fit for this specific container." The better the fit, the less likely the students' brains are to see the scheme and resist it.

There is one personally relevant issue that merits special mention, because it is such a dependably successful container for so many different types of content. It is called *fun*. Here's how fun works. When teachers design learning experiences

Human beings, it seems, are particularly interested in themselves…

Nothing in this world can take the place of persistence. Talent will not: nothing is more common than unsuccessful men with talent. Genius will not; unrewarded genius is almost a proverb. Education will not: the world is full of educated derelicts. Persistence and determination alone are omnipotent.

- Calvin Coolidge

that not only produce content mastery, but are also fun, they are partnering with a powerful ally. Inside the human brain, fun is not just fun. Fun is survival linked. The human brain is designed to master quickly and remember well anything that is linked to personal survival (LeDoux, 1996, 2003). Fun is linked, very linked. So, when teachers make a learning experience fun, they are strategically increasing retention and transfer, and decreasing the need for review and re-teaching. Fun makes for more efficient and more memorable learning. Fun is survival linked and survival drives human attention and deep learning. Fun is not just fun. Fun is also cheese (Rutherford, 2009c).

Recently I was watching a high school Spanish teacher conduct a lesson on grammar. It was the day after Valentine's Day. She organized the class into teams and asked each team to submit a Valentine's Day card with an original, romantic metaphor in Spanish. Each team then shared their work and the class voted on the best romantic line. It was hilarious! They reacted to each effort with applause or groans. The winner was, "On the highway of love, you have a lot of curves and I have no brakes." What fun! Make no mistake; they were getting the grammar right. The fun made it faster, easier, and more memorable (Rutherford, 2009c).

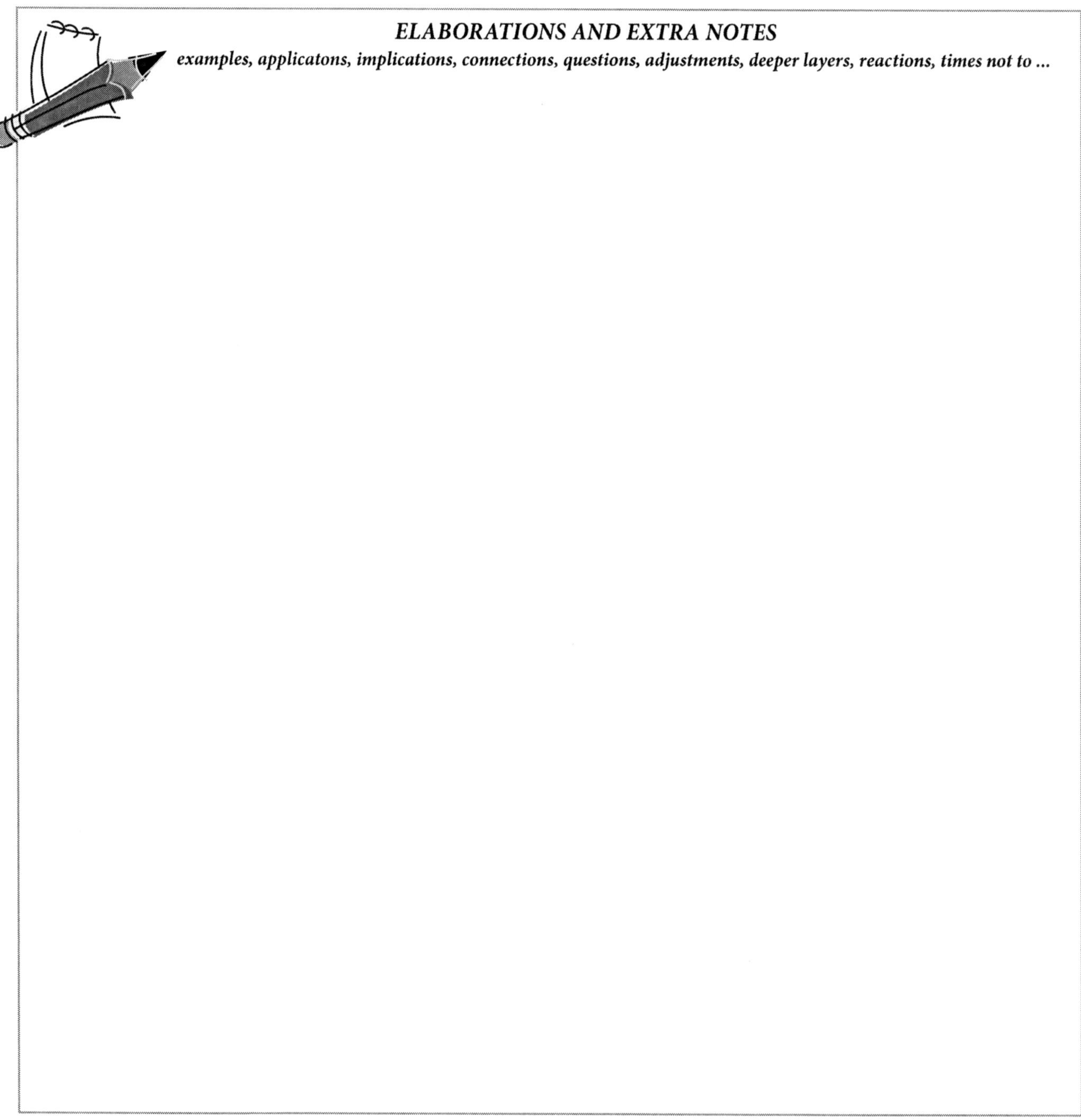

ELABORATIONS AND EXTRA NOTES

examples, applicatons, implications, connections, questions, adjustments, deeper layers, reactions, times not to ...

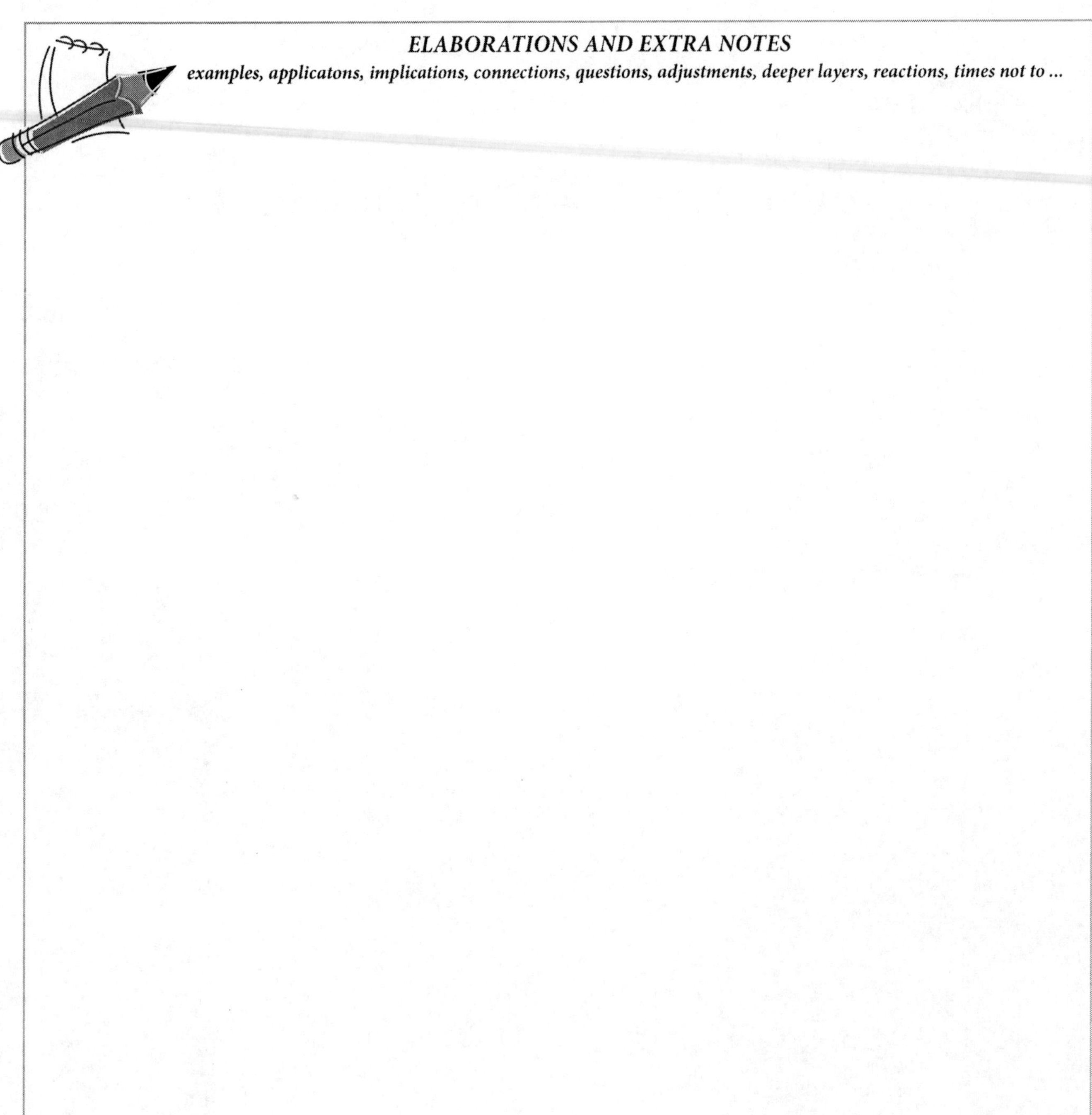
ELABORATIONS AND EXTRA NOTES
examples, applicatons, implications, connections, questions, adjustments, deeper layers, reactions, times not to ...

THEME 12A

Locale Memory

I've never let my school interfere with my education.
- Mark Twain

Locale Memory

Definition. The ability of the teacher to enhance learning by organizing information around the learner's position or "locale" in three-dimensional space.

Elaboration. Memory is enhanced when concepts, skills, or information is encountered in a relational manner, not as a series of unrelated or disconnected facts (Cohen and Eichenbaum, 1993). Human beings are endowed with an innate and powerful ability to function in and navigate through the natural, physical world (O'Keefe and Nadal, 1978). As a part of our survival apparatus, we can remember how to get home, where that bee's nest is (to avoid a sting), where the coffee is to be found in the grocery store, or how to play hop-scotch. When we lose our car keys, we retrace our steps to find them. We might say to a friend, "watch your six," invoking the layout of a clock face to suggest he keep an eye on who's behind him.

When classroom information is presented in a physical, spatial context, this innate navigational ability is tapped to the great benefit of recall and transfer of learning. (Caine and Caine, 1994).

Fine art is that in which the hand, the head, and the heart of man go together.
– John Ruskin

A math teacher who constructs a large scale version of the X-Y coordinate plane on a gym floor and then asks students to stand in quadrant II is invoking locale memory.

A science teacher who lays out the planets' relative distances from the sun on the football field, showing that Jupiter is many, many times farther from the sun than the Earth, is using locale memory.

A history teacher who walks students down the timeline of World War II, constructed in the hallway with tape and sticky-notes, is teaching to students' local memory systems.

When a student looks at her right hand, palm up, and remembers where key cities are in the state of Michigan, she is using her locale memory system.

A fifth grade teacher uses locale memory as she takes students outside to the 36' x 48' United States map that the PTO painted on the school playground. The teacher asks students to use chunky blue chalk to draw in the major rivers. When all the students are finished, each group has to "walk" the entire class down their river, identify the states they pass, and share other facts about the river.

A Spanish teacher uses locale memory by linking vocabulary words to a scavenger hunt. He divided the class into groups of three and gave each group a starting clue. The clues were in Spanish and sent the students to various locations and people around the school. Some clues led them to inside an empty locker, under the school mascot, above the visitor sign in the lobby, etc. Other clues involved school personnel such as the school nurse. When the students went to the person, they received another clue that instructed them to sing, jump, bark, or some other action before they could receive the next location clue. All the clues eventually led the students back to the classroom for the scavenger prize... a dish of flan. As the students enjoyed the treat they were complaining and laughing about the places they went and actions they performed, such as: Cante Centelleo, Centelleo, Estrella Pequeña para el secretario.

A high school Physics teacher uses locale memory to review Newton's laws of motion, center of gravity, momentum, rotational inertia, torque, and the coefficient of sliding friction. The teacher takes the students to a nearby elementary school playground. The swings, slide, monkey bars, jump rope, and balls are the instructional materials. As the students interact with the playground equipment, the teacher reviews applicable physics laws. The following day, student groups make a poster of an assigned playground item. On the poster, they record the physic laws that were demonstrated at the playground. Throughout the semester, the teacher often refers back to the playground adventure, "Remember when you..."

Information that is not anchored to a physical, spatial context takes more time to learn, requires frequent rehearsal to keep it current, and must be limited to small amounts. Great amounts of information can be stored in locale memory. It can be quickly learned and requires little review to maintain access (Caine and Caine, 1994).

Information that is not anchored to a physical, spatial context takes more time to learn, requires frequent rehearsal to keep it current, and must be limited to small amounts.

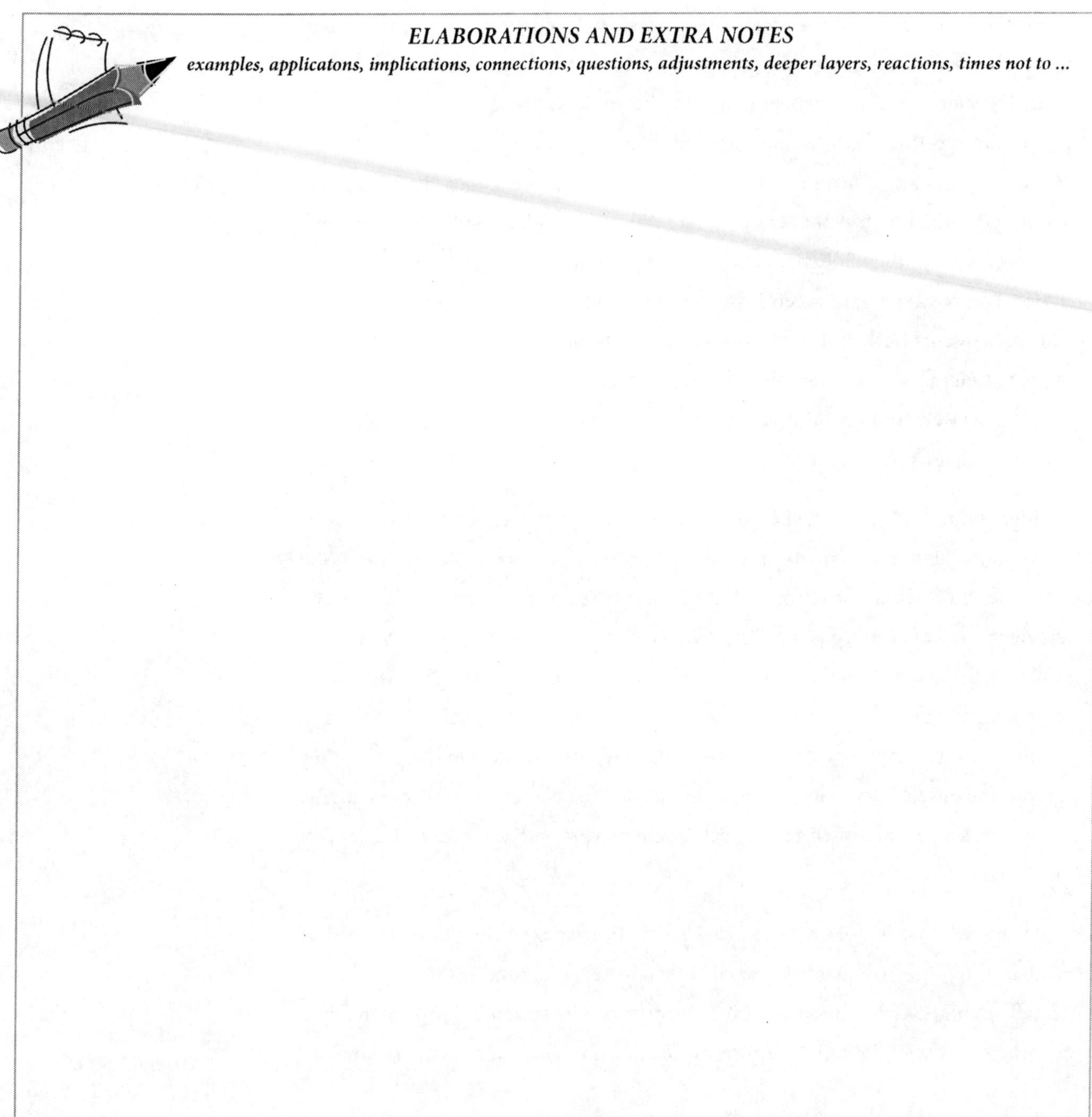
ELABORATIONS AND EXTRA NOTES
examples, applicatons, implications, connections, questions, adjustments, deeper layers, reactions, times not to ...

THEME **13**

Mental Models

Mental Models

Definition. The ability of the teacher to provide a memorable structure that organizes, clarifies, and improves recall of the content being taught.

Elaboration. Mental models support the learner's need to clarify and position the content in memory for recall. Venn diagrams, T-charts, and bubble maps are mental models. Songs, stories, jingles, rhythms, and sayings are mental models. Smells, sounds, textures, and tastes are mental models (Mastropieri & Scruggs, 1998).

The neuroscience behind mental models points to the role of hemisphericity, the difference in the way the two brain hemispheres process information (Ali & Kor, 2007). It is an oversimplification of the brain's structure and function to exclusively assign specific learning tasks to either hemisphere. As a general guide, however, consider that the left hemisphere tends to process text, language, logic, and symbols while the right hemisphere tends to process images, intuition, emotions, and sensory input (Springer & Deutsch, 1993). Mental models enhance clarity and recall by associating a right hemisphere process (for example- the colors of the

Useful mental models should help the learner clarify the content as well as remember it.

rainbow) with a left hemisphere process (for example the text-ROY G BIV). The two processes together provide an architecture for the brain to better consider, and remember, the intended content (Boyle & Weishaar, 1997; McCarthy, 1987). Useful mental models should help the learner clarify the content as well as remember it. Notice that the mental model ROY G BIV not only provides a way to remember the colors of the rainbow (Red, Orange, Yellow, Green, Blue, Indigo, Violet), but also adds clarity to the content by listing them from longer to shorter wavelength in the same sequence, left to right, that the colors appear in nature.

I don't want to be interesting. I want to be good.
– Ludwig Mies van der Rohe

Visual mental models are particularly effective when used to increase comprehension of text. Robert Marzano (2007) and David Hyerle (1996) point out that classroom learning is enhanced with the use of visual representations. Marzano, Pickering, & Pollock (2001) call these types of mental models non linguistic organizers. Pairing a text (linguistic) item with a visual (non linguistic) structure creates a memorable structure on which learners can assemble and recall information (Larkin & Simon,1987).

Mental models are also constructed by linking sensory representations (right hemisphere processing of sights, sounds, textures, smells, or tastes) to symbol systems (left hemisphere processing of letters, words, numerals, or > < ? + % ∞ ° A=πr^2) (Arcavi, 1994; Ghazanfar & Schroeder, 2006). Teachers of young children often ask them to trace the letter b on the sand table as they say it. This creates a powerful processing link between the two hemispheres. A music teacher might write these terms for tempo on the board: allegretto (moderately fast), allegro (brisk or rapid), and presto (very fast). Then the teacher might provide an audible structure by singing the letters of the term allegretto moderately fast, the letters of allegro briskly, and the letters of presto very fast.

Some of the most powerful mental models link left and right hemisphere processing, or ways of thinking. A Geometry teacher might ask students to predict which geometric solid, a cone or a pyramid, has the greatest volume. Predicting, or identifying a hunch or guess, is mostly right hemisphere thinking. Then, the students fill the shapes with colored water to see which holds the most. The process of measuring and recording the actual volume in milliliters is a left hemisphere process. An art teacher might, before the students begin their two-week paper mache project, ask them to examine several completed projects from last year. The left hemisphere processes the sequence of steps in the project while the right hemisphere processes the gestalt of the finished projects.

Mental models are found extensively in children's literature. Notice, in a well illustrated book for young children, how the text and the illustrations are often close together or even superimposed. The images provide a structure to which the simple words can attach.

Democracy cannot succeed unless those who express their choice are prepared to choose wisely. The real safeguard of democracy, therefore, is education.

– Franklin D. Roosevelt

Mental models are evident in the field of advertising. Well-crafted logos, jingles, and tag lines create memorable associations with products, services and brands.

Mental models are often used effectively in wise sayings, idioms, proverbs, or parables. Visual or symbolic imagery makes it easier to pass on wisdom from one generation to the next as illustrated in these sayings: "A bird in the hand is worth two in the bush" and "The early bird gets the worm."

Teachers who employ a wide variety of mental models will likely find the theme Locale Memory (Theme 12) to be an effective complement. Locale memory is, essentially, a mental model that is constructed in the physical domain instead of the cognitive domain. A Venn Diagram, for instance, can provide an effective structure for organizing similarities and differences. In order of increasing impact from the physical domain, the Venn Diagram can be made of two, partially overlapping circles on a piece of notebook paper, big circles on a piece of poster paper, two hula hoops overlapping on the floor, or two big circles drawn with paint on the playground. Each increase in scale increases the positive contributions of spatial, or locale memory (Caine & Caine, 1994).

A writer should write with his eyes and a painter paint with his ears.

– Gertrude Stein

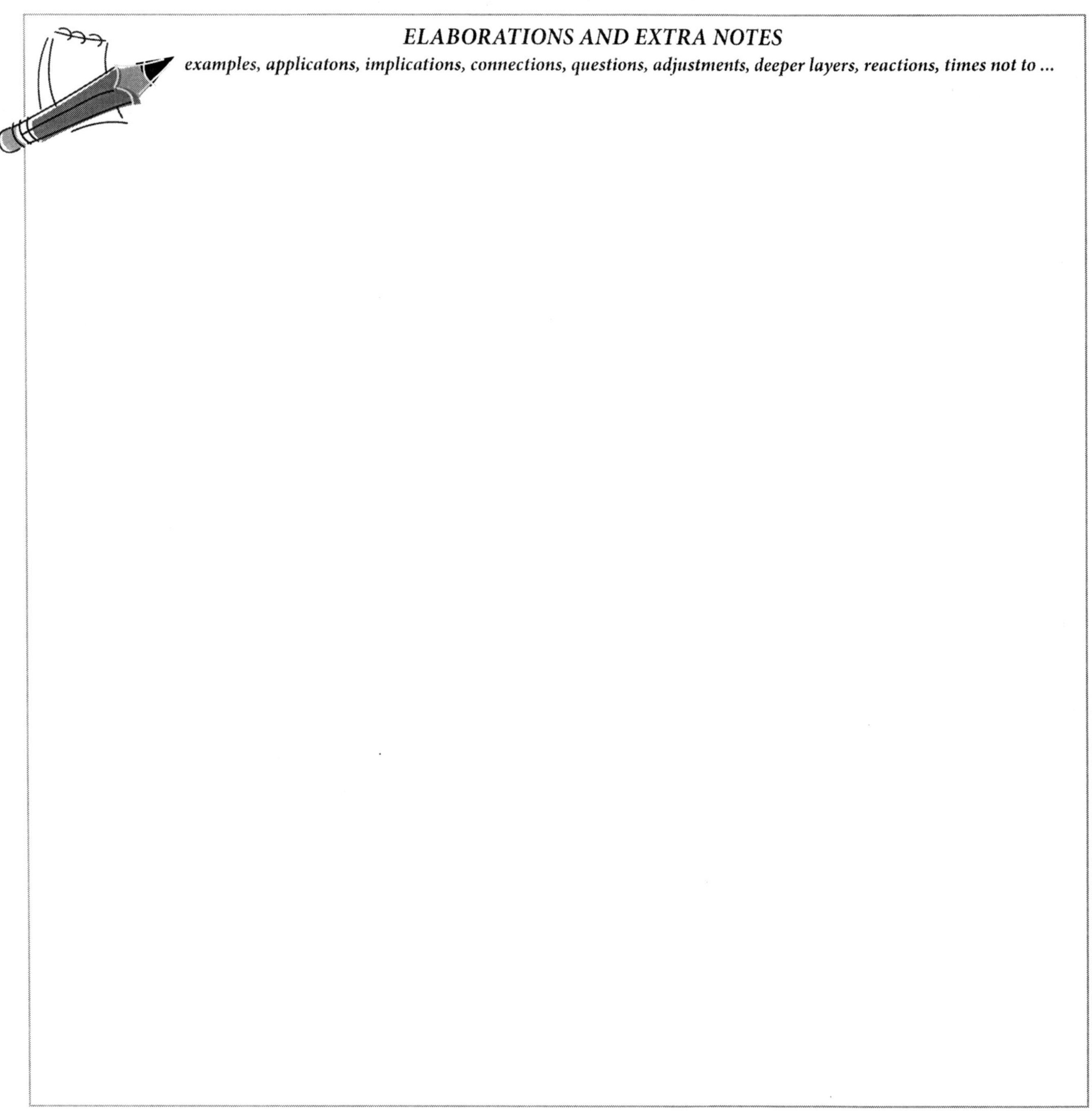

ELABORATIONS AND EXTRA NOTES

examples, applicatons, implications, connections, questions, adjustments, deeper layers, reactions, times not to ...

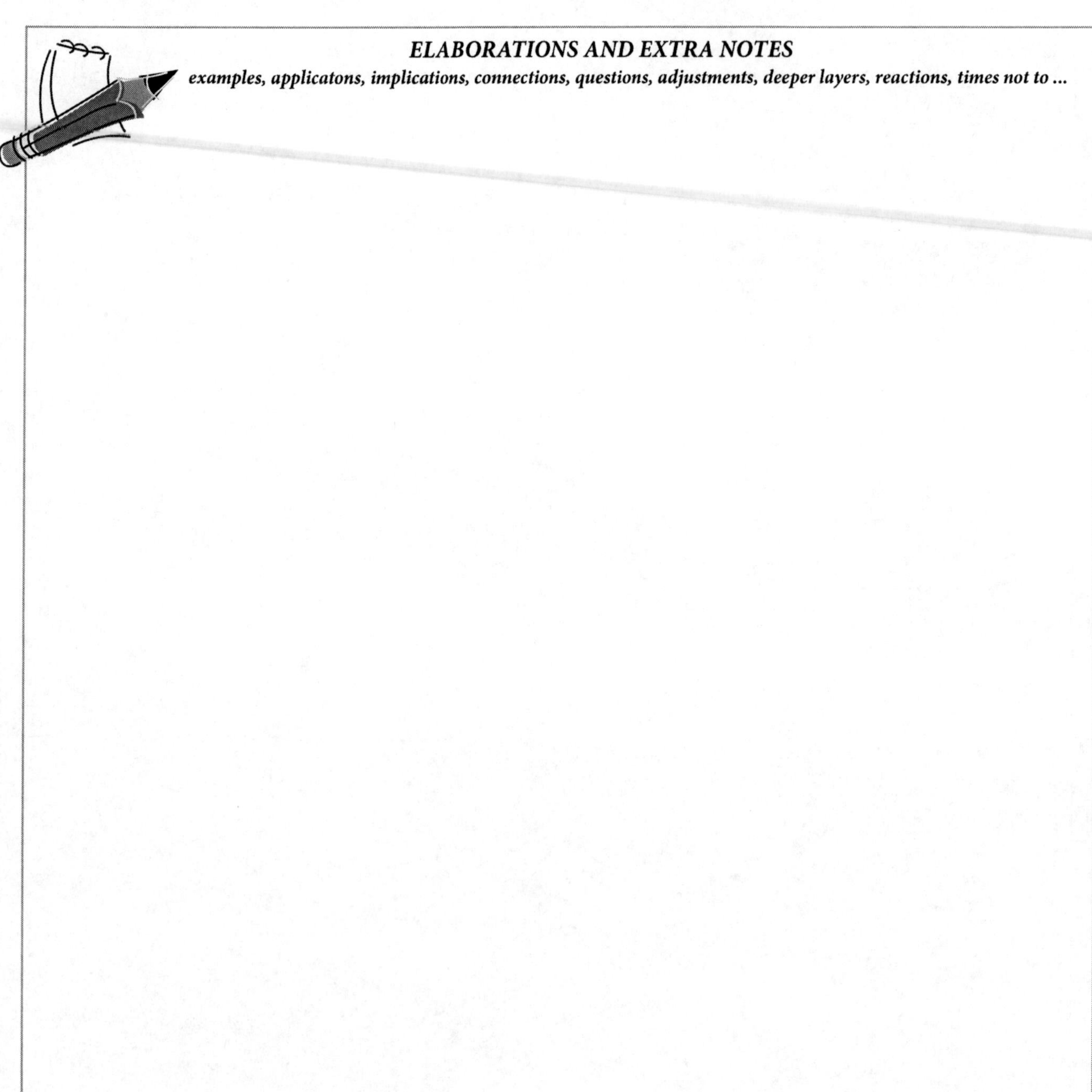
ELABORATIONS AND EXTRA NOTES
examples, applicatons, implications, connections, questions, adjustments, deeper layers, reactions, times not to ...

THEME **14**

First Time Learning

First Time Learning

Definition. The ability of the teacher to capitalize on the brain's tendency to attend to, process deeply, and remember well, learning it regards as new, original, or novel.

Elaboration. First impressions stick with us. Do you remember your first memories of the ocean, or the Rocky Mountains, or ice cream? How about your first car, your first crush, or your first ride on the tilt-a-whirl? There is something about initial experiences that just has more staying power in our memories. This staying power can work for us or against us. If we learn to factor binomial equations well the first time through (remember FOIL- first, outside, inside, last) it sticks with us, but if we learn someone's name incorrectly when we first meet them, we might always have trouble recalling their correct name.

First time learning also influences our attitude about various activities (Martin & Clore, 2001). If our first camping trip was a lot of fun, we might go again and even become avid campers. If our first experience was just insects, rain, and boredom, then we'll probably opt for a hotel.

Life is painting a picture, not doing a sum.
- Oliver Wendell Holmes

There is something about initial experiences that just has more staying power in our memories.

Teachers who are adept at corralling the memory effects of first time learning understand that these effects cannot be turned on or off at the teacher's discretion. They just happen. They happen whenever a learner's brain encounters something for the first time, whether the teacher is ready for it or not. In some ways employing first time learning starts with anticipating it, planning for it, or at least not being surprised by it.

The experiential and anecdotal evidence that supports the presence of a first time learning effect is substantial. We've all experienced these effects and can recall examples from our own learning and from our experiences teaching others. The cognitive science behind first time learning is still emerging, but these three explanatory approaches appear to lead the way, each with a slightly different emphasis.

First time learning as a survival function. This approach maintains that the primary function of the human brain is to maximize the probability of survival in the surrounding environment. The brain loves music, a good sitcom, and conversation with engaging friends, but its primary function is survival, to get us to the next few moments of life. New experiences then are extraordinarily pertinent to this function. When exposed to a situation we've seen before, the brain knows how to respond since it has experienced the situation and has some history to draw from as to how to survive, or even capitalize on the event. When the brain encounters something new, not possessing a reference pattern, it pays rapt attention to the new information or experience to quickly assess its importance and whether it has positive, negative, or neutral implications for survival. It is this rapt attention and the emotional responses that accompany it that drives the positive memory and learning effects we see with first time learning (Cahill, Gorski & Le, 2003).

It may seem odd to consider that students' brains are on survival watch while they are at school. I suppose some classrooms might possibly bore someone to death. But, other than the occasional hallway fight, is there really a serious question of survival in the classroom? Evolutionary biologists would remind us that we all engage in a 21st century life using brains that evolved over millennia to aid our survival in a very different environment (Caine & Caine, 1994). When a teacher says "Today we'll learn a brand new term for an important element of writing. I'll bet you've never even heard this word before. It's called onomatopoeia," the students' brains react just as their ancient, hunter-gatherer ancestors' brains reacted to the discovery of a tasty new fruit- examining it with full attention to determine whether it might be nourishing or poisonous.

First time learning as a function of imprinting. Imprinting, in the natural world, refers to the attachment an animal makes in the early moments of its life to its parents or the first reasonably similar object it encounters (Bateson, 2003) (Hess, 1973). A compelling example of this is documented in the 1996 movie *Fly Away Home*. The movie, which was inspired by a true story, documents the lives of a flock of orphaned Canadian Geese who imprint upon the young girl who cares for them. She uses an ultra-light airplane to teach them how to fly south for the winter.

Imprinting is the biological correlate of a cognitive process called assimilation (Sluckin, 1965). In assimilation, the brain uses new information to construct a sort of mental architecture on which subsequent learning can be attached. In both cases, these powerful early memory effects are associated with early experiences or initial learning. Just as described in the previous section on first time learning as a survival function, there appears to be extra attention paid to first or early experiences. This extra attention and memory serves as a sort of category heading to which future learning and experience can be associated (Bhattacharya & Han, 2001).

There is no end to education. It is not that you read a book, pass an examination, and finish with education. The whole of life, from the moment you are born to the moment you die, is a process of learning.

- Jiddu Krishnamurti

A man who carries a cat by the tail learns something he can learn in no other way.
– Mark Twain

First time learning as a function of primacy and recency effects. Perhaps one of the aspects of first time learning that has been best documented is the ability of the brain to better recall items that are learned first in a series (primacy effect) or last (recency effect). Conversely, the hardest to remember items in a list tend to be found in the middle of the sequence, where neither primacy nor recency work to enhance memory (Sousa, 2011). It is more likely that the average person can remember the first two presidents and the last two presidents than the 23rd president (Benjamin Harrison). The first presidents occupy a "category heading" in our minds with which subsequent presidents are associated, but probably not remembered. The last presidents are remembered because it is easier to remember things that happened recently and also because these presidents are likely to be more directly relevant to our lives. Again, first place counts for recall.

As teachers plan for first time learning, they can maximize the positive effects by focusing on these four instructional criteria:

Accuracy. Since first time learning will yield long-lasting memories, it is important to get it right the first time. Spell words correctly the first time they are presented. Pronounce them correctly. Provide the correct definition and usage. If teaching the tennis backhand stroke, show the correct form first, not common errors. A teacher should not begin instruction on the correct use of semicolons by asking students to correct sentences where they are misused. The teacher who works a complex math problem a few times the night before to be sure it is right ensures positive first time learning.

This is not to say that students can't benefit from discovery learning or inquiry learning, where the "right" answer is elusive at first. Just be careful to watch for negative first time learning and be sure that students grasp the concept accurately before the cement dries.

Completeness. Introduce first time learning content when there is sufficient time and energy to provide a successful first experience (Bransford, Brown, & Cocking, 2000). New concepts should not be introduced during the last few minutes before the end of the school day, or just before lunch, or as a time filler between other scheduled activities. Teach first time learning in prime time, when interruptions are less likely and minds are fresh.

Also, it is important to bring closure to a first time learning experience at a strategic point, not just when time runs out. A useful analogy is found in culinary arts class where the teacher must be sure to end the lesson at a strategic time when the food can "keep" overnight. There are similar points in all academic lessons where the learning can be "kept" overnight and added to later.

Connected to reality. The first day of Mr. Sullivan's 9th grade woodworking class is spent at the local lumberyard, not in class. He wants to ensure that the first time his students hear the term "4x8 sheet of plywood," they are actually looking at one and examining the layers of wood that are called plies.

The context of initial learning is important (Bransford, et al. 2000). As a general rule for first time learning, don't use representations of reality when actual reality is available. A diagram of a microscope produces poorer first time learning than an actual microscope. A video of a raccoon is better for first time learning than a drawing of a raccoon, but not nearly as memorable as a live raccoon.

Interestingly, representations of reality can be very productive and efficient for subsequent experiences, after an initial experience that is closely linked to reality. That diagram of a microscope makes perfect sense after the student has had a quality first experience with a real microscope. So, the sequence is important. It's reality first, then representations of reality following.

Genius without education is like silver in the mine.

– Benjamin Franklin

I cry out for order and find it only in art.
– Helen Hayes

Different from subsequent lessons. Initial learning is most memorable when it is presented in a substantially different form than the following experiences. The purpose of an effective introduction to new material is to create a memorable experience that sets the stage for subsequent experiences (Gagne, Briggs, & Wagner, 1992). It need not, and probably shouldn't, seek to teach all the detail or ask students to engage in repetitive rehearsal activities.

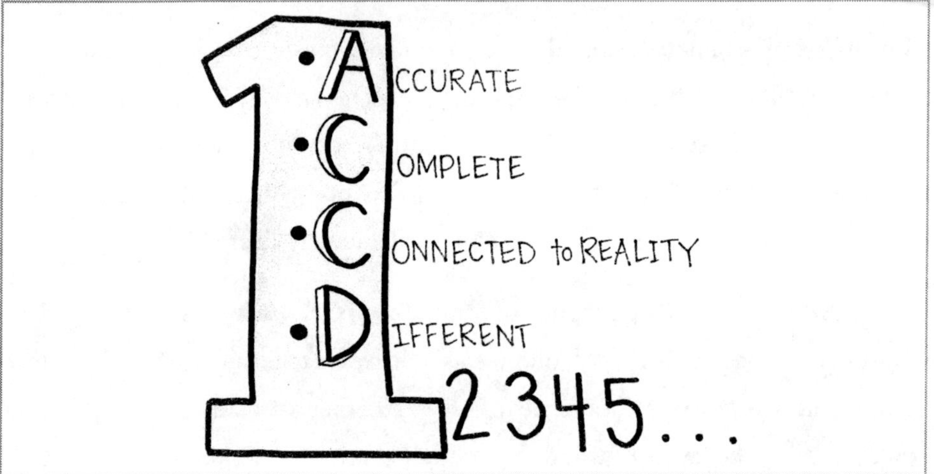

A language arts teacher might ask a parent who is a terrific story teller to dress in costume and read the class a riveting story and record the story on video. After the story, the teacher might ask students to identify what made the story so easy to listen to, funny, and memorable. Recording the responses on a flip chart, she might then circle some of their comments and label the responses with the term hyperbole. The teacher could then replay segments of the story and ask students to identify other instances of hyperbole and note when the laughter was loudest. Notice that the introductory lesson is more elaborate than later lessons on hyperbole need be. The teacher, recognizing that this is a first time learning moment, created an experience that was accurate, complete, connected to reality, and substantially different from lessons that will follow. Introductory lessons are good investments of extra planning time, materials, and classroom energy.

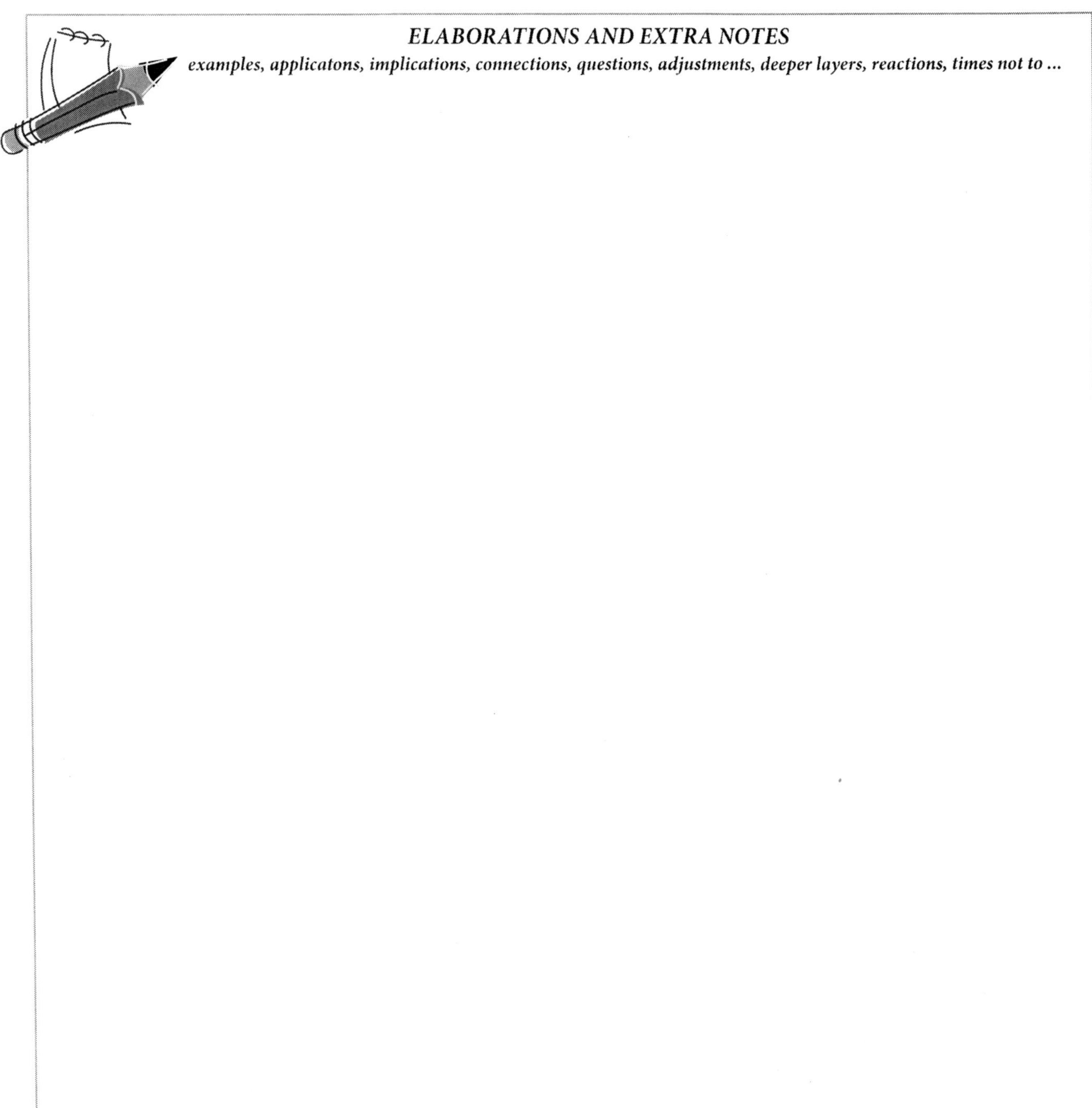

ELABORATIONS AND EXTRA NOTES

examples, applicatons, implications, connections, questions, adjustments, deeper layers, reactions, times not to ...

ELABORATIONS AND EXTRA NOTES

examples, applicatons, implications, connections, questions, adjustments, deeper layers, reactions, times not to ...

THEME 15A

Neural Downshifting

Neural Downshifting

Definition. The ability of the teacher to prevent "survival mode" thinking by eliminating physical threats, psychological threats, and situations where students feel helpless or out of control.

Elaboration. Neural downshifting refers to the negative effects of threat and stress on human thinking and learning. This phenomenon is sometimes called fight or flight response, threat response, or survival mode thinking.

The term "neural downshifting" was first used by Leslie Hart in his 1983 book, *Human Brain and Human Learning*. Hart writes, "Thus we have the phenomenon, readily observable in ourselves and others, including students, that I have called 'downshifting.' When the individual detects threat in the immediate situation, full use of the great new cerebral brain is suspended, and faster acting, simpler, brain resources take larger roles" (Hart, 1983, p.108). Hart's understanding and description of neural downshifting is based, in large part, on Paul MacLean's triune brain theory (MacLean, 1978). Triune brain theory suggests that the human brain's thought processes can be understood as the interplay among three

To make us feel small
in the right way is a
function of art;
men can only make us feel
small in the wrong way.
– E. M. Forster

progressively newer (in evolutionary terms) brain systems. MacLean refers to the oldest brain structures as reptilian, the next, newer systems as old mammalian, and the newest as new mammalian (1978). Downshifting then, is the threat induced *shifting* of thought from the rational, creative new mammalian structures of the brain down to the faster, but simpler structures below.

New technologies and new research over the decades since MacLean's work have provided a vastly richer picture of the brain's neurophysiology and MacLean's triune brain theory has received both notoriety and criticism over the years (Cory & Gardner, 2002; Pinker, 2002; Reiner, 1990). Placing the paleocerebral arguments aside, the essential insight that the human brain operates optimally in an environment free from threat and undue stress has endured, and in fact has been reconfirmed (Caine and Caine, 1994; Damasio, 1994; LeDoux, 1996; Jenson, 2008).

In the classroom, downshifted thinking is characterized by rote memorization, reflexive responses, and unoriginal approaches. Upshifted thinking is

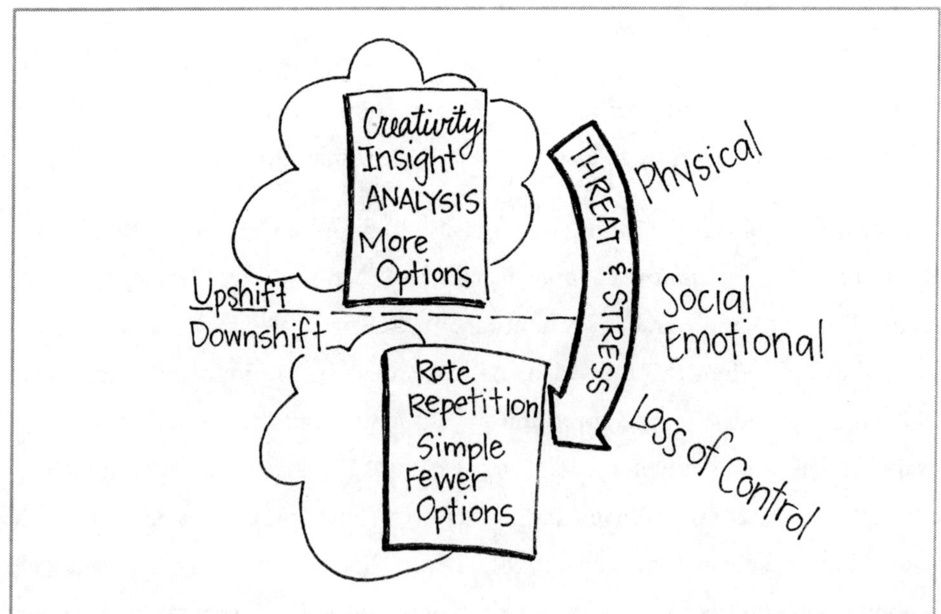

If someone is going down the wrong road, he doesn't need motivation to speed him up. What he needs is education to turn him around.

– Jim Rohn

characterized by creativity, analysis, cooperation, pattern recognition, and insight (Caine & Caine, 1994; Hart, 1983).

Unlike the other twenty-two Artisan themes, neural down-shifting refers to something that is to be avoided in the classroom. A teacher who understands the effects of neural downshifting and the environmental triggers which cause neural downshifting, can take steps to prevent it from occurring.

Three environmental triggers of neural downshifting.

Downshifting will occur in the presence of a *physical threat* (Hart, 1983). Certainly, fighting and bullying cause downshifting. So, also, do other less obvious physical factors such as overcrowding, hunger, thirst, confinement, fever, exhaustion, and being too hot or too cold. Teachers do well to examine their classroom's physical environment and eliminate physically threatening situations.

Downshifting will occur in the presence of *social or emotional threats* (Jenson, 2008). The old saying "sticks and stones may break my bones, but words will never hurt me" may be true in a purely physical sense, but words, or any other social or emotional threat cause the same downshifting response as do physical threats. Teachers do well to examine their classroom's social and emotional characteristics and remove threats. Being wrong in public, forced competition, time constraints, fear of recognition, fear of social blunders, and overt comparisons among students are all examples of social and emotional downshifters.

Downshifting will occur in the presence of *helplessness or loss of control* (Caine & Caine, 1994). This is perhaps the most subtle, but pernicious, cause of classroom downshifting. It seems that the brain will downshift into safe mode when it perceives that it is out of control of the immediate situation. Firefighters, police officers, and emergency room doctors score high on job stress measures. Studies have shown that the stress levels of copilots often exceed that of pilots and

The human brain operates optimally in an environment free from threat and undue stress.

that middle managers suffer more stress than CEO's. Why is this? The common thread that runs through these examples is that they are all high stakes-low control occupations. It is interesting that in the above occupations, training is emphasized. This makes sense. While downshifted, as one would be in a house fire or a police shootout, one cannot create new, original approaches, but must fall back on learned and practiced responses.

One, almost universally effective antidote to loss of control downshifting is *choice*. When teachers provide students with options, choices, and personal decisions, their sense of ownership and control is increased and downshifting is reduced.

It is important to note that neural downshifting is not a phenomenon that affects students only. Teachers and administrators, when confronted with physical, social, or loss of control triggers, will suffer neural downshifting too. It is hard to imagine a school where downshifted adults can dependably create upshifted environments for students.

Art begins with resistance - at the point where resistance is overcome. No human masterpiece has ever been created without great labor.

– Andre Gide

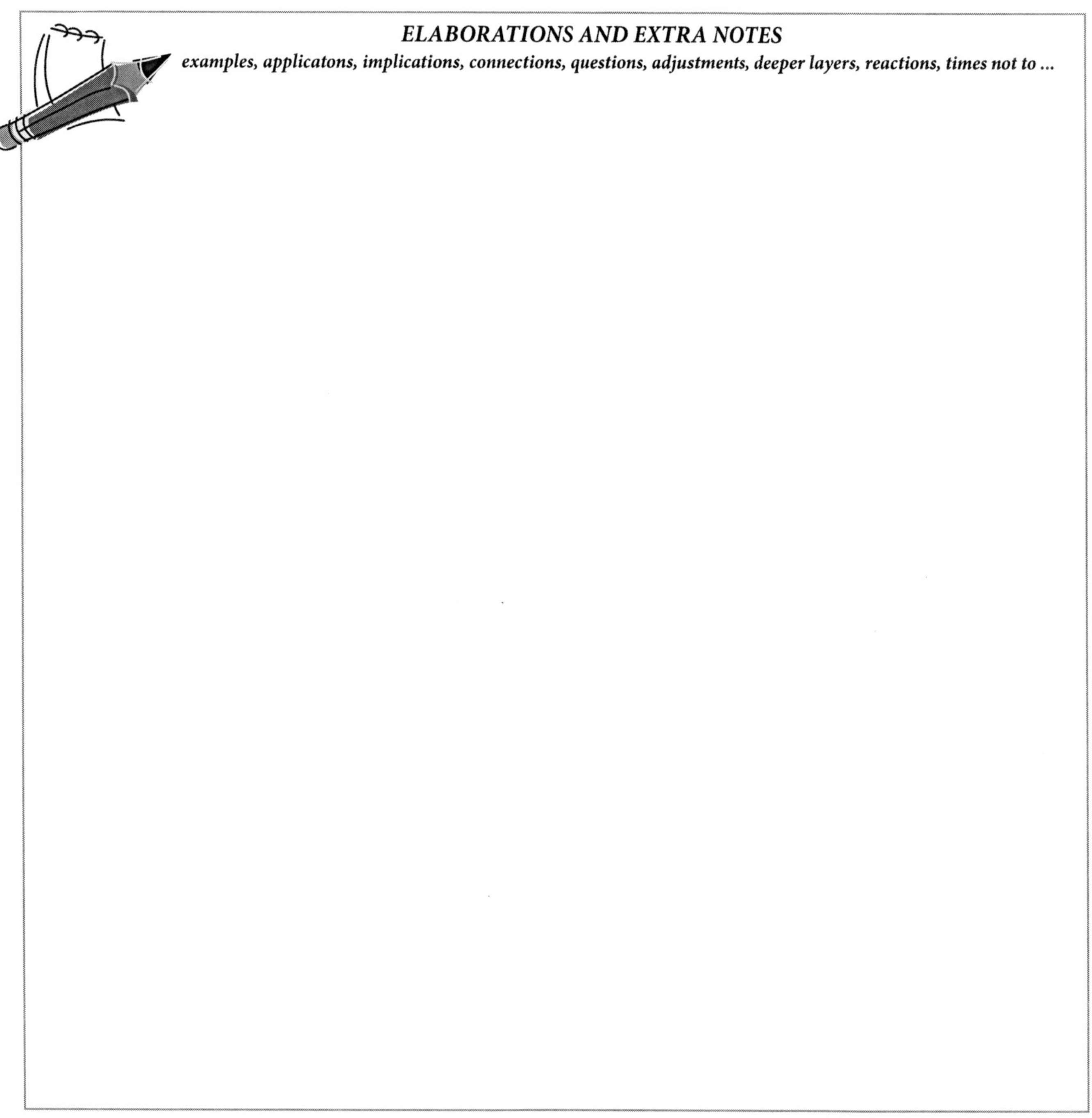

ELABORATIONS AND EXTRA NOTES

examples, applicatons, implications, connections, questions, adjustments, deeper layers, reactions, times not to …

ELABORATIONS AND EXTRA NOTES

examples, applicatons, implications, connections, questions, adjustments, deeper layers, reactions, times not to ...

THEME **16**

Enriched Environments

Classroom environments are more enriched when there are things to do in the classroom, not just places to sit.

Enriched Environments

Definition. The ability of the teacher to shape the physical and social environment of the classroom to enhance learning.

Elaboration. One of the most exciting scientific discoveries of the past 50 years, and one with significant implications for educators, is that the human brain does not contain a fixed number of brain cells, but rather, can generate new neurons and new connections among neurons throughout our lifespan (Diamond, 1984). Neural plasticity, the ability of the brain to change its physical form and function to match the needs of the environment (Van Pragg, Kemermann, & Gage, 2000) provides the foundation for this consideration of classroom environments, and how they might affect, for better or worse, the learning and achievement of students.

The scientific examination of the effects of environmental enrichment on the human brain and human learning is still incomplete. Much is not known about exactly which environmental conditions are responsible for specific brain changes or when, in the lifespan, these changes are most pronounced, or if, and how,

Music is the movement of sound to reach the soul for the education of its virtue.

– Plato

these brain changes affect human intelligence, learning, and school achievement (Huttenlocher, 2002). Still, the exciting brain research on neural plasticity and the effects of enriched environments provide some broad insights into how enriched environments work (Diamond, 1984) and how teachers might design classroom environments for the benefit of students and their learning.

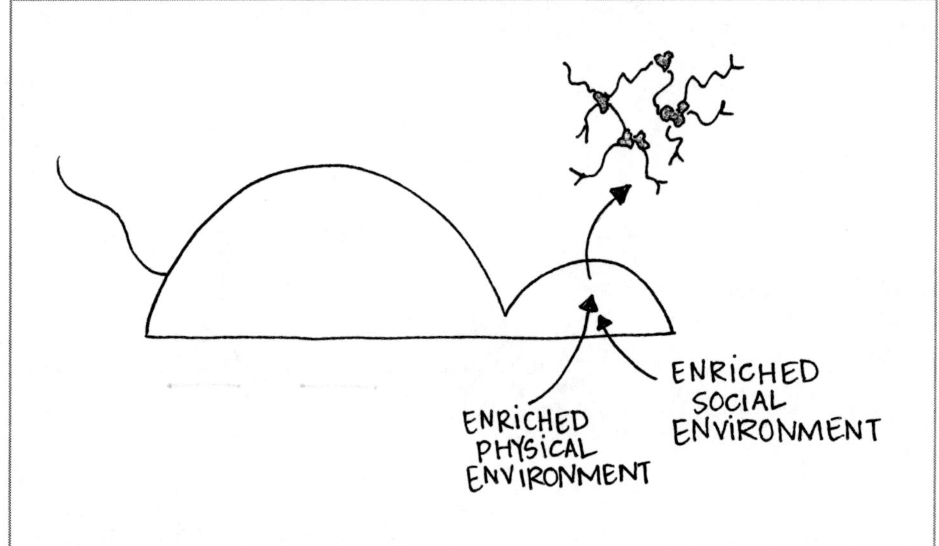

Much of the research on the brain effects of enriched and impoverished environments has been conducted by placing groups of rats in environments with different characteristics and then looking at the rat's brains to see what, if any, effects are evident (Huttenlocher, 2002). The environmental characteristics most consistently associated with positive brain effects were (Diamond, 1984; Diamond, Johnson & Ingham, 1971):

- Rats were placed in larger cages with more rats in each cage. This increased the amount and complexity of the social relationships among the rats.
- The physical environment was changed frequently with new toys, new layouts, and new opportunities to engage with the environment. This

"periodic novelty" increased the learning required for rats to engage with the environment.

- The environment encouraged increased physical activity by providing running wheels, tunnels, ladders, and space to move. This increased the overall physical activity of rats as compared to the control group.

Informed by thousands of classroom observations, and in keeping with the three broad themes of environmental enrichment from the rat studies (social complexity, novel physical environment, and increased physical activity), here are some guidelines for creating enriched classroom environments. Note that enriching elements are found in both the physical environment and in the social environment of the classroom.

Physical characteristics of an enriched classroom environment.

Opportunities for physical engagement. Classroom environments are more enriched when there are things to do in the classroom, not just places to sit. A place to cast a vote for your favorite adjective, a place to leave a sticky note of positive feedback on others' writing samples, a place to estimate the number of jelly beans in a pickle jar, a place to use yarn and push pins to show connections between Spanish and English terms, a place to quiz yourself on ACT vocabulary words, a place to check your heart rate, do 30 jumping jacks, and then check it again to note the change, a place to check the outside temperature and record the data are all examples of elements that enrich the physical environment of the classroom.

Note that in all cases, there is a physical location designated for the activity, the activity involves some degree of physical action, there is an element of novelty to each activity, and that the activities are relevant to the curriculum.

FIELD NOTES:

Rules and models destroy genius and art.

- William Hazlitt

Education comes from within; you get it by struggle and effort and thought.

– Napoleon Hill

Periodic changes in the physical environment. Without question, there should be areas of each classroom's physical layout that are consistent throughout the school year. It would be foolish to change the location of the fire drill procedures or to send in a work order to change the location of the classroom sink. And, there is a level of familiarity with the classroom layout that enhances classroom management and reduces stress. Beyond these management considerations, however, there is usefulness in change. Change that creates new requirements for thinking, new sequences to remember, new people with which to interact, new materials to encounter, new media to master, new visual angles to interpret, or new habits to learn cause the brain to adjust and grow to handle the new challenges at hand.

Changes in the physical classroom environment can be simple or subtle and still produce a novel effect. The process can also be systematized. Many teachers create several locations in their classroom that they know will be changed on a regular basis to match the changing curriculum, leaving the rest of the classroom layout to be consistent.

Social characteristics of an enriched classroom environment.

Unconditional positive regard. The term "unconditional positive regard is generally attributed to Carl Rogers, a humanistic psychologist who believed that, during counseling, people experienced more growth in an environment of genuineness, acceptance, and empathy (McLeod, 2007).

On the first day of school, parents everywhere ask their children the same question, "Do you like your teacher?" I have a theory. I believe that when students respond to that question, the question they are really answering is "Does my teacher like me?" As the year progresses, some other relevant questions are answered too. "Is my teacher glad I'm in the class?" "Does my teacher think I'm an important member of the group?" "Would my teacher miss me if I was absent?" "Would my teacher want to be around me if he didn't have to?" When these internal questions are answered mostly in the affirmative, students experience UPR, a powerful enriching element of the classroom environment.

Relaxed alertness. Learning is optimized in an environment of safety and security where the nervous system is relaxed and not overwrought with stress or anxiety. Learning is also optimized when there is internal motivation, interest, heightened awareness, alertness, and energy. When the classroom environment is characterized by both of these states simultaneously, the stage is set for high quality engagement and deeper learning (Caine & Caine, 1994).

Elite athletes often model relaxed alertness in their performances. Usain Bolt, the Jamaican sprinter who, at this writing, holds the world record for the 100m dash at 9.58 seconds, is unquestionably alert and fully engaged as he runs. Look closely though, and you will see that he is also relaxed, calm, and almost serene as he cruises past his competition. He actually seems to be enjoying the experience, rather than fighting the wind for that last tenth of a second.

Michele Wie, a LPGA golfer, also models relaxed alertness. As she addresses the ball for a tee shot, she is smooth and fluid, never jerky or overextended. Somehow, out of that smooth, effortless swing, comes the golf ball exploding through the air for another 300+ yard drive. She is one of the most powerful ball strikers on tour, but also one of the smoothest. She is both at the same time.

In the case of athletes and students, the goal of relaxed alertness is not to create a balance between relaxation and alertness, but rather to have as much of both as possible, to be very relaxed and very alert, simultaneously.

A second-grade teacher moves from station to station, encouraging students to engage in the various reading drills with their best efforts. Music plays in the background and students are smiling, laughing a little, and enjoying the practice work. They are relaxed and alert.

Art is science made clear.
- Wilson Mizner

You can't legislate good will - that comes through education.
- Malcolm X

A Spanish II teacher tests and records students' fluency with timed readings. She sets the clock for 60 seconds and says, "Go." Students read as quickly as they can, but with fluency and expression. They don't panic when they come to a difficult word, but simply do their best and move on. Before each trial the teacher encourages students to relax and breathe naturally. "You'll do better, if you're conversational and at ease." She assures the students that they can take the timed test as many times as they'd like and they can keep their best time. Almost every student makes gains from their previous test. They are relaxed and alert.

Special treatment. Have you ever made a request of someone in an official position and heard a response like this, "I'd really like to help you with this, but if I did, I'd have to do the same thing for everyone who might ask. And, since I can't do that, it wouldn't be fair to do it for you."? How did that make you feel? What if the person replied like this: "I can see that you're one of our most loyal customers. I'm, technically, not supposed to do this, but I'll take care of it just as you asked. Thanks for your business." How would that make you feel?

In essence, special treatment is a signal that one is a member of a group, and that membership in the group occasionally affords one benefits not available to non-members. You've experienced the sensation of special treatment if you've ever received a warning ticket from a police officer, or if you've ever been late to work and the boss just winked and said, "Don't make a habit of it." Loyalty programs operate on the principle of special treatment. Frequent flyers enjoy benefits not available to all fliers. Grocery stores offer special savings to those who possess a loyalty card. In so doing, these companies cement a bond of membership with consumers. There is a sense of reciprocity in these relationships that benefits both the consumer and the provider.

Mr. Sigmund, a ninth grade Language Arts teacher, called Josh to his desk one afternoon. "Josh, I was able to score two free passes to the movies for this weekend. I overheard you saying you would like to go. Why don't you take these and enjoy a show?" "Wow thanks! What did I do to deserve this?" asked Josh. "Nothing really," replied Mr. Sigmund, "It's just a perk of being in the best ninth grade Language Arts class in the school!"

In the classroom, when teachers signal to students that they are members of a special group (our class), they create a more enriched environment characterized by a mutual sense of connection and reciprocity.

Positive rituals. Just like special treatment, the effect of positive rituals is to signal group membership. Military units have special ceremonies to commemorate a completed mission, or a new deployment. Churches employ rituals such as baptism, communion, or call and response readings to promote unity in the faith. Sports teams have special elbow bumps, or high fives to signal group membership. Positive rituals are repeated reminders that one is a member of a special group. Knowledge of the ritual and exactly how it is to be performed is limited to the members of the group.

Mr. Johnson, a fourth grade teacher, responds to an especially thoughtful student response by inviting students to give the responder a "fantastic." The students all point their fingers like they are holding a bottle of Fantastic, the cleaning spray, and say, "Squirt, squirt." They then make a circular motion with their other hand as if wiping with a paper towel and say, in unison, "Squeak squeak." This is a positive ritual, a repeated gesture that is unique to the group. It identifies those who know it as group members and excludes those who do not know the technique. Mr. Johnson has many more positive rituals that he has taught his students and they alternate using them throughout the day. It's as if Mr. Johnson has created a secret society in his classroom, where students are bound by blood oaths of loyalty and commitment. Little do they know that fourth graders right

To send light into the darkness of men's hearts - such is the duty of the artist.

– Robert Schumann

across the hallway and also across the nation are all saying "squirt, squirt, squeak, squeak" in response to extra good answers.

More collaboration, less competition. Enriched social environments are characterized by collaboration. Classroom environments are more positive when students are working with one another to achieve learning goals rather than competing against one another for scarce rewards or recognition (Kohn, 1999). This is not to say that a little classroom competition is always harmful. Many an afternoon are made more productive by a "boys vs. girls" quiz game or a team sharks vs. team dolphins math competition. Competition creates energy and energy is necessary for engagement and learning. Still, on balance, classroom environments are more enriched by a spirit of family, togetherness, team spirit, and unity.

A true, and sad, story: I was observing a ninth grade English classroom one morning and noticed that the students were sitting according to an unusual seating chart. Students were seated according to their test averages. There were thirty seats in the classroom arranged in six rows of five. The #1 position, reserved for the student with the highest average was in row 1, seat 1. The student with the lowest average sat in row 6, seat 2 (there were 27 students, total). I asked the teacher how this impacted the classroom environment. She said she believed it motivated the students and that they appreciated knowing exactly where they stood. I was stunned. As I reflect on that experience, I believe the teacher was correct, in a sense. Fear of failure and constant comparison to others can be motivating, just as hunger can motivate a person to find work. A classroom with a truly enriched social environment, however, seeks to motivate students through the inherent value in learning, the fun of working together, and the positive energy that flows from being a part of a high performing team.

Experience is simply the name we give our mistakes.

– Oscar Wilde

A final note on collaboration and competition: In the rat research, the enriched environment cages were set up to avoid competition for basic needs. All the rats had all the food, water, space, nesting material, and access to toys they needed. It was the complex social relationships that developed among rats, in the absence of competition over basic needs, that appeared to increase dendrite density and brain development (Diamond, 1984). Perhaps we could learn a lesson from the rats.

The principles of true art is not to portray, but to evoke.

– Jerzy Kosinski

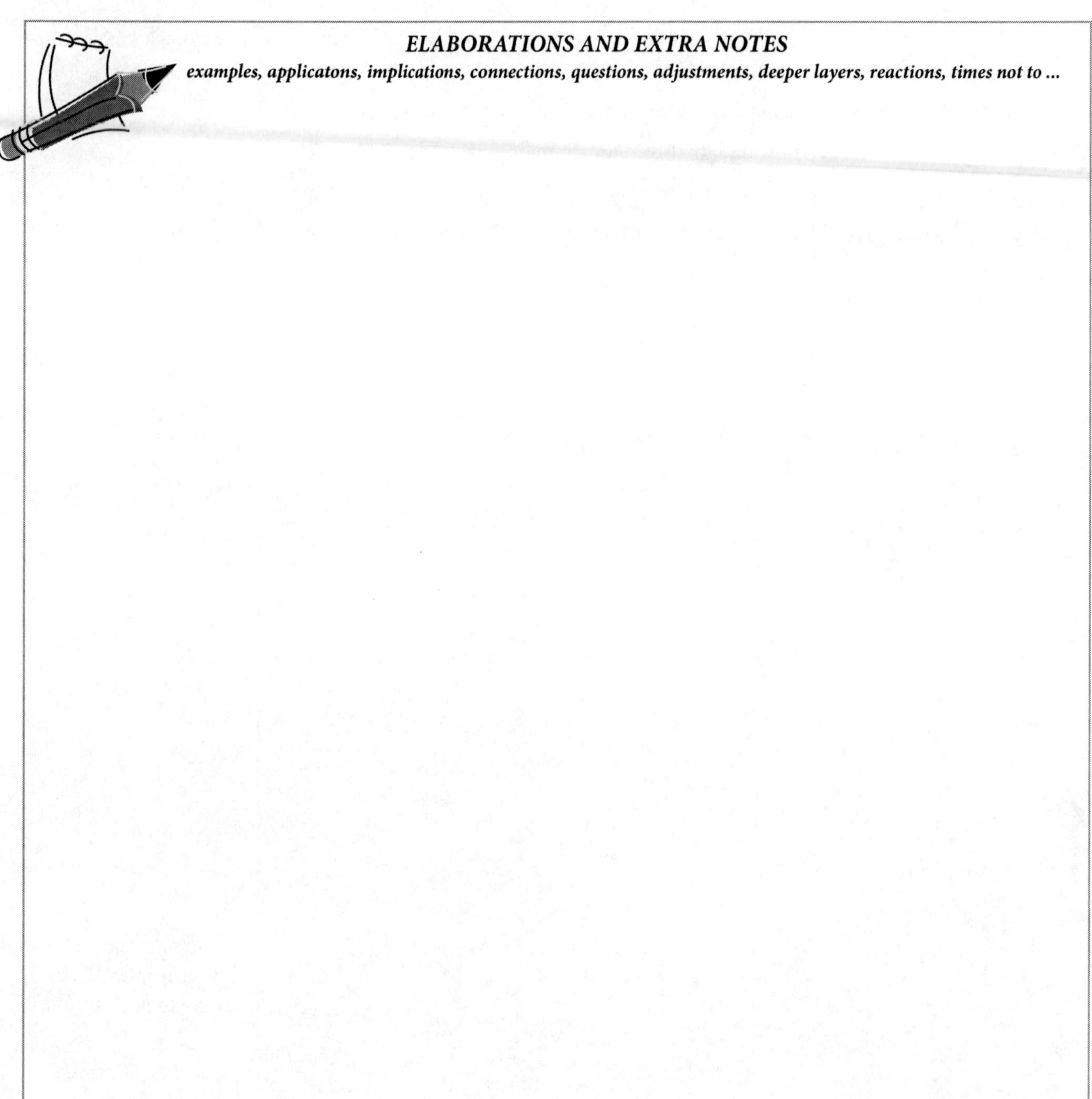
ELABORATIONS AND EXTRA NOTES
examples, applicatons, implications, connections, questions, adjustments, deeper layers, reactions, times not to ...

THEME 17

SUCCESS

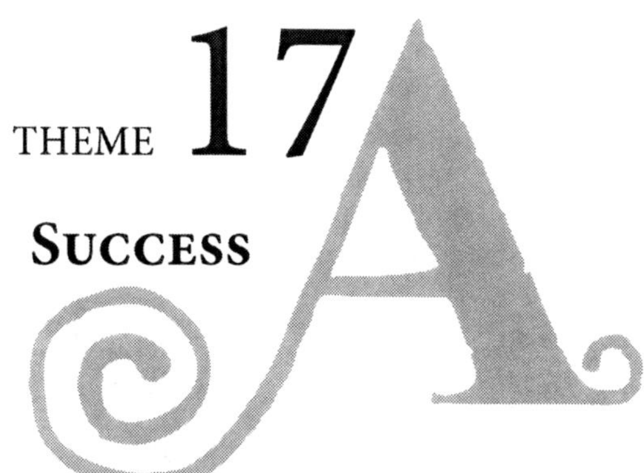

The only real failure in life is one not learned from.
– Anthony J. D'Angelo

Success

Definition. The ability of the teacher to increase and sustain student effort by designing and adapting learning tasks to ensure that students experience success.

Elaboration. Success and effort are linked. When students give great effort to a learning task, they are more likely to be successful. And, when students experience success at a learning task they are more likely to give effort (Cummings, 1992). Effort and success, then, are mutually reinforcing. They comprise a positive feedback loop. Effort leads to success, which in turn, leads to even more effort, which leads to even more success. Of course, the loop can move in the opposite direction too. Low effort leads to failure, which in turn, leads to even less effort, which in turn, leads to even more failure.

Madeline Hunter describes student success as a key to student motivation. She explained that teachers play an essential role in designing and creating student success. Hunter (1982) wrote,

> You may wonder how you can affect students' successful achievement. Isn't that a result of the students' ability and effort? In part, yes. But student success

> is also responsive to two other factors which you control. The first is the level of difficulty of the learning task, something you can adjust since you set the task. The second factor is your teaching skill which will make students' learning more probable (p. 14).

The Hungarian psychologist, Mihaly Csikszentmihalyi, suggests that a state of flow, or optimum experience, is possible when a balance is struck between the challenge of the task and the skill of the performer. This flow state, similar to being in the zone or in the groove, is intrinsically motivational and is characterized by a sense of immersion or absorption in the task at hand (Csikszentmihalyi, 1990).

Student effort is affected by the student's expectation for success and also by the degree to which students see value in that which they are learning (Feather, 1982). To receive full effort, a learning task must be seen as doable and also meaningful. Students will withhold effort from learning tasks they see as trivial, unimportant, irrelevant, or uninteresting (Feather, 1992). Effort is affected by the value of the task itself (inherent value) and by the value of the consequences of performing, or not performing, the task (consequential value) (Feather, 1982).

To receive full effort, a learning task must be seen as doable and also meaningful.

The relationship among effort, success and value can be expressed as a mathematical equation: Effort = Expectation of Success x Value (Cummings, 1992).

Effort. A student's effort can be described as the product of two factors- aptitude and persistence.

Aptitude is the student's learning rate (Carroll, 1963). A student with a high aptitude for music, for example, can learn musical concepts and skills faster than a student with a lower aptitude for music. Aptitude is determined by, among other variables, how much background knowledge and experience a student already has in an area of study (Gardner, 1983). *Success tip:* Engage students through areas of higher aptitude. A student with a high verbal aptitude might be more successful if allowed to record a persuasive paragraph before writing it down. A student with high kinesthetic aptitude would do well to "act out" the solving of a binomial equation rather than just considering the problem mentally (Gardner & Hatch, 1989).

Persistence is the student's level of "stick-to-it-iveness." Students who are able to persist in a task for an extended period will, on balance, learn more. Aptitude and persistence are interdependent since the lower a student's aptitude, the longer he will require (persistence) for mastery. *Success tip:* Provide students more time for mastery. Lower aptitude students, especially, simply need more time to achieve success. This can be accomplished by providing more time, providing additional practice sessions, shifting time from other activities, adding before and after school opportunities, or applying advanced teaching/learning strategies that accomplish more in less time.

Expectation for Success. A student's expectation of success is determined by two factors: perception and prior experience.

Success is not final, failure is not fatal: it is the courage to continue that counts.

– Winston Churchill

Education is the leading of human souls to what is best, and making what is best out of them.

– John Ruskin

Perception is the degree to which the learning task looks doable. Teachers can alter a student's perception of a task by positioning the task to appear easier, more approachable, or similar to a familiar task. *Success tip:* Manage student perceptions. A difficult math problem from page 367 in the textbook, can look less intimidating if it's presented by itself, written with a marker on a piece of construction paper. Working in a group of four, rather than by oneself, can make tough assignments seem less so. Breaking a long project into separate parts and focusing students' attention on just the next part can make the work seem less daunting.

Prior Experience. Success breeds success. Students gain momentum and a sense of self-efficacy when they accomplish tasks successfully (Brophy, 1987). Often, the best predictor of student effort is to check the recent past to look for instances of success. *Success tip:* When a teacher ensures that students are consistently successful, the momentum from prior successes carries over to current work.

Value. The value that a student sees in a learning task is the sum of its inherent value and its consequential value.

Inherent Value. Inherent value refers to the enjoyment and importance found in the work itself, not in external rewards or sanctions (Kohn, 1993). *Success tip:* Rely mostly on inherent value of learning tasks. Point out to students how much they enjoy reading, how they always like to solve hard problems, or how they are so good at coming up with novel ideas. Motivation is stronger and longer lasting when it is embedded in the work itself (Csikszentmihalyi, 1990).

Consequential Value. Consequential value refers to the value that a student places on a positive consequence of giving effort to a task, or the avoidance of a negative consequence due to the withholding of effort from a task. *Success tip:* Use consequential value temporarily, perhaps only initially, until inherent value can be realized. Withdraw consequences as soon as possible so as not to limit student effort to the minimum levels required to gain rewards or avoid sanctions.

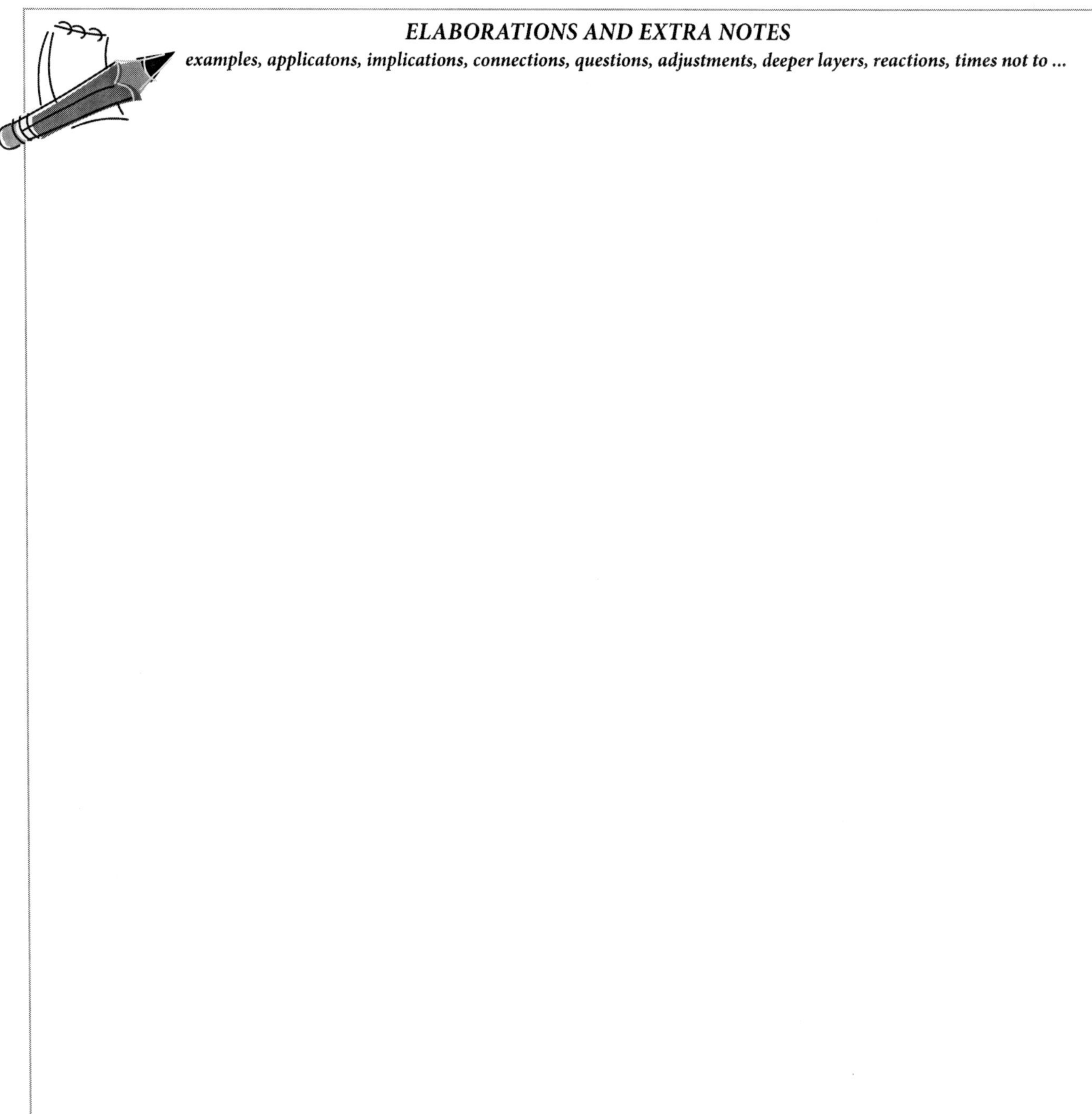

ELABORATIONS AND EXTRA NOTES

examples, applicatons, implications, connections, questions, adjustments, deeper layers, reactions, times not to ...

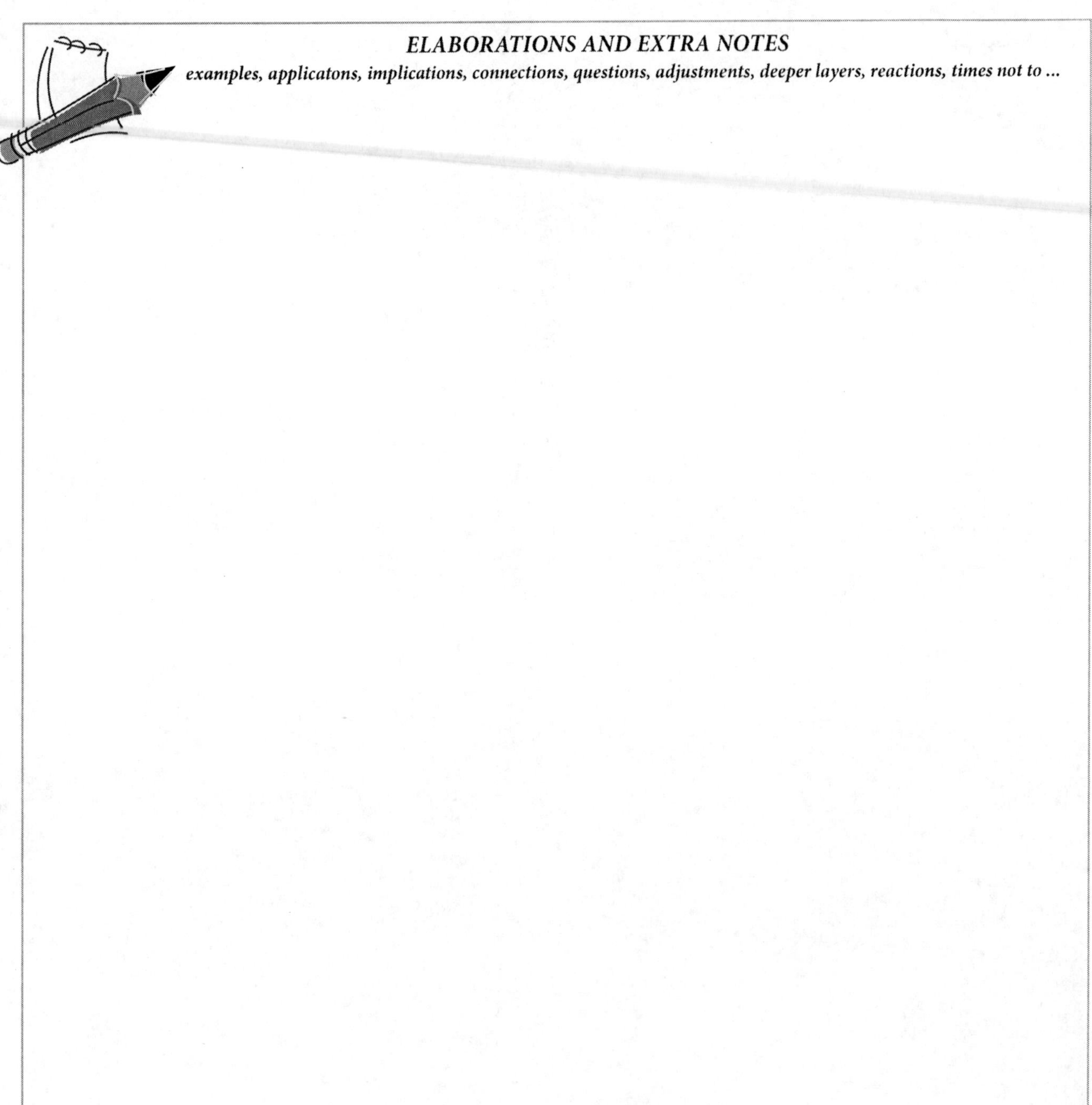
ELABORATIONS AND EXTRA NOTES
examples, applicatons, implications, connections, questions, adjustments, deeper layers, reactions, times not to ...

THEME 18

PERFORMANCE FEEDBACK

FIELD NOTES:

Performance Feedback

Definition. The ability of the teacher to increase students' mastery of and persistence at a task by providing abundant, immediate, and specific knowledge of results.

Elaboration. Timely and specific performance feedback is an important ingredient in the recipe for student learning. Feedback allows learners to quickly self-adjust their performance, which is conducive to mastery (Sousa, 1995, p. 45). Beyond this direct benefit to mastery, performance feedback also delivers another, complementary effect- persistence.

When the brain is engaged in a recurring loop of practice-feedback-adjustment, it seems to not mind exercising the loop again and again. This "stick-to-it-iveness" effect sometimes manifests itself in a temporary loss of time awareness (Csikszentmihalyi, 1990). One can lose track of time during a good conversation with a friend, an interesting internet search, or a favorite video game. All three of these activities activate the brain's "do something-receive something back-do something again" response- persistence.

Success consists of going from failure to failure without loss of enthusiasm.
- Winston Churchill

Although not completely understood, the basic mechanism behind this increase in persistence is likely to be chemical in nature. The Canadian neuropsychologist Donald Hebb proposed in 1949 what is now known as Hebb's axiom: "Neurons that fire together wire together" (Hebb, 1949). During repeated performance feedback loops, electrical and chemical energy courses through neural networks reinforcing networks that receive positive feedback and re-wiring networks that do not yet produce the desired result. This process of repeated reinforcing and revising of networks causes chemicals to be synthesized and released causing a positive, pleasant sense of well-being.

In a sense, the brain is being chemically rewarded for doing its work. This chemical release-reward loop is one way of understanding how performance feedback can cause persistence in the task at hand. "Current research suggests that the brain is capable of making its own rewards. By producing and releasing natural opiates and endorphins, the brain can create a natural high." (Kaufeldt, 1999, p. 187).

Art is the stored honey of the human soul, gathered on wings of misery and travail.

– Theodore Dreiser

Success principles for performance feedback.

As teachers plan to provide performance feedback to their students, it is helpful to consider these three attributes of effective performance feedback.

Abundant feedback, rather than scarce feedback. Learning is optimized when feedback is torrential (Jenson, 1998, p. 43). Most people with reasonable athletic ability can learn to snow ski in a single day. Why? Because every muscle and nerve in their feet, legs, and torso is receiving feedback multiple times each second on how to stay upright and move down the mountain. Soon they can ski well enough to enjoy the rest of the day. The feedback is abundant.

Immediate feedback, rather than delayed feedback. The positive effects of learning feedback are multiplied when the feedback loop is fast (Hattie & Timperley, 2007). When hours or days pass between the trial, the feedback, and the next trial, feedback is still valuable, but the reinforce/revise loop is interrupted and therefore the momentum for learning is lost. A good rule of thumb is that feedback should return to the learner within the time they can hold their breath.

Specific feedback, rather than vague or generalized feedback. In order to gain the benefits of performance feedback, it is important that the feedback be "actionable." Actionable feedback provides not only a general judgment of the work, but describes a specific element of the work that can be immediately reinforced or revised. Let's say students are writing persuasive paragraphs and the teacher is moving from student to student providing feedback. "Nice work!", "B-", or ☺ provides only a general judgment of the work. More specific, actionable, feedback sounds like "Your first sentence is attention grabbing. That's nice work" or "I'd like for you to have a least three elaborations on your opening statement. You have one, and it's a good one. Add two more that are just as interesting."

Successive Approximation. There is a special category of performance feedback that maximizes the reinforcement/revision process. Successive approximation is learning through quick, repeated practice with small adjustments toward a goal. The psychologist B.F. Skinner first used the term successive approximation in detailing his theory of operant conditioning (Skinner, 1937). A Spanish teacher

No effective puppy trainer would ever give a dog a treat and say "by the way, that was a good fetch you did yesterday."

The true sign of intelligence is not knowledge but imagination.
– Albert Einstein

employs successive approximation when he asks a student to practice the rolling r sound as in the word roho (Spanish for red). The teacher and student go back and forth, each saying the word, perhaps a dozen times, until the student can say it just right. When students are engaged in this type of feedback they are perhaps never more motivated and engaged as they get closer and closer to the goal with their teacher right there guiding them.

Some insights on performance feedback can be gained by considering how it works outside a typical classroom.

Puppy training. In puppy training, it is crucial to deliver the treat immediately after the puppy, performs the desired behavior. The feedback must be immediate. No effective puppy trainer would give a dog a treat and say "By the way, that was such a good fetch you did yesterday."

Golf lessons. In golf instruction, teachers often use video replays to help the student see the specific intricacies of the golf swing. Rather than saying, "That's a nice swing. Keep it up," the instructor might pause the video to point out exactly how the student's left elbow is positioned. Then the instructor might say, "When you keep your left elbow tucked in close to your body, your swing stays on plane just fine." The specificity of the feedback enhances learning.

Language learning. One of the best and fastest ways to learn a new language is to be totally immersed in the location, language, and culture where the language is spoken. An immersion experience provides such abundant feedback that the learning is rapid, relevant, and memorable.

Video game design. Game designers know the effects of abundant, immediate, and specific feedback to the player and they design it into every level of every game. It is a compliment to the game designer for a player to say "I couldn't put it down."

ELABORATIONS AND EXTRA NOTES
examples, applicatons, implications, connections, questions, adjustments, deeper layers, reactions, times not to ...

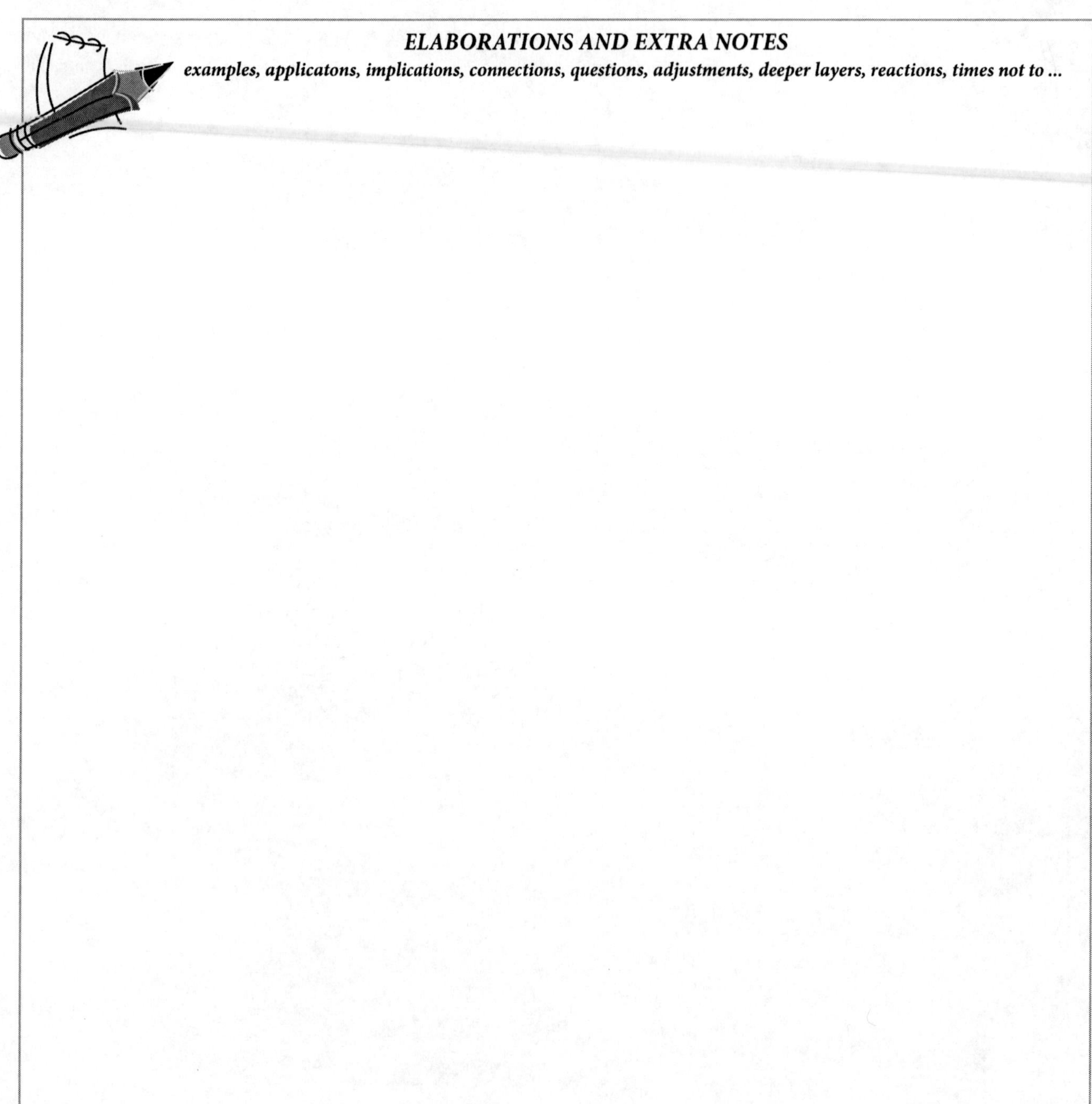

ELABORATIONS AND EXTRA NOTES

examples, applicatons, implications, connections, questions, adjustments, deeper layers, reactions, times not to ...

THEME **19**

STAGECRAFT

Good teaching is one-fourth preparation and three-fourths pure theatre.

- Gail Godwin

Stagecraft

Definition. The ability of the teacher to enhance, deepen, or prolong student engagement by utilizing a theatrical treatment such as props, music, lighting, scenery, choreography, body position, voice, music, costumes, and visual/ audio effects.

Elaboration. Sometimes the difference between an effective lesson and an unforgettable lesson is the way the teacher captures and keeps the learners' attention and interest using techniques borrowed from theater. Teachers can make lessons significantly more impactful and memorable by applying theatrical elements.

There is much to learn in observing how actors ply their craft, how choreographers create a symphony of experience, how expert set designers create engaging scenery, how great lighting focuses attention, and how a good musical score highlights an unforgettable performance (Rutherford, 2009a, p. 1). When theatrical techniques are employed skillfully and in the right combinations, the audience is transported

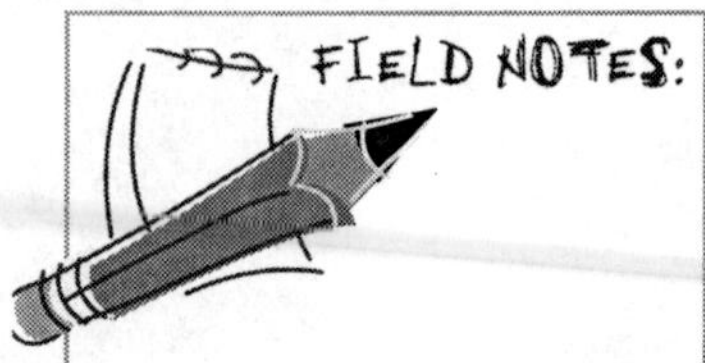

The ability to enhance and transform another's attention has great utility in the theater and also in the classroom.

through a momentary suspension of disbelief (Coleridge, 1817), to a far-away place or into the mind of an interesting character. This ability to enhance and transform another's attention has great utility in the theater (Grainer, 2010) and also in the classroom.

As teachers borrow theatrical techniques for the purpose of enhancing students' attention, it is helpful to think in terms of applying a theatrical *treatment*. A treatment is a specific classroom application of a specific theatrical technique. A treatment does not add to or alter the curriculum standard or the purpose of the teacher's lesson, but rather highlights aspects or segments of the lesson by causing the learner's mind to linger a bit longer, ask a few more questions, or process in a slightly deeper or different way. The treatment might be the way an object or area is lit, it might be a prop that grabs attention, or it might be the way the teacher moves throughout the classroom space.

To be sure, classroom teachers are not expected to be perpetual actors on the classroom stage, and every lesson need not be "performed" to be effective. It is the technical aspects of theater such as lighting, props, or staging that have the most import to the classroom, not the acting skills of the teacher.

Stagecraft, then, is mostly about the applications of technical theater to the classroom. Not every moment of instruction needs a theatrical treatment and a teacher should not feel compelled to add a treatment at every turn. Sometimes, though, it is the treatment that opens the door for the learner's mind to create and cement a more elaborate understanding of the information presented. Teachers can employ, when needed, specific treatments to lengthen student's attention spans, deepen their observation skills, or create a particularly hard to forget classroom moment.

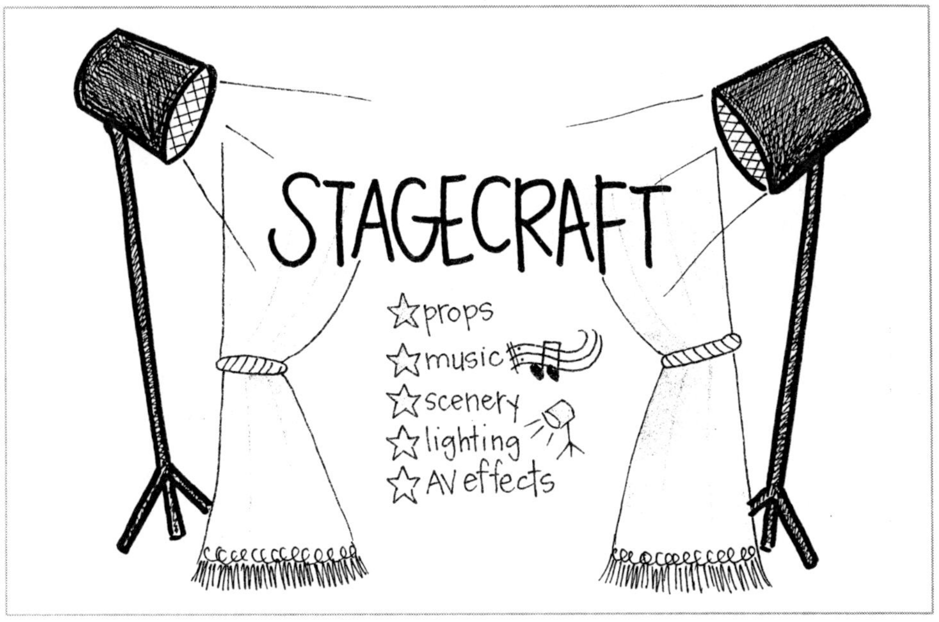

Some elements from technical theater include.

Props. Short for "property of the theater company," props are artifacts from the scene and setting of a performance that add credibility to the story (Richardson, 1996). A pirate is more believable with a cutlass in his teeth, Moses looks more like himself with a scroll in hand, and the quiver of arrows is a key signal that the man in green tights is indeed Robin Hood. Likewise, the Geography teacher who holds a globe while teaching latitude and longitude makes a more memorable point. The teacher can go a step further by distributing small, inflatable globes to all the students so they can trace for themselves the prime meridian, equator, and Arctic Circle.

Lighting. The lighting director knows that the audience's eyes, and therefore their mind and mood, will follow and fix onto what is lighted. "Light the talent" is one of the basic principles of lighting design (Pilbrow, 1991). Teachers can apply this principle by paying attention to classroom lighting- keeping key areas and key

I would rather entertain and hope that people learned something than educate people and hope they were entertained.
– Walt Disney

One eye sees,
the other feels.
– Paul Klee

people in the light. For added effect, inexpensive LED spot lights (best with a flexible gooseneck and clamp) can draw attention to a flip chart or a display area.

Scenery. The human brain has a great capacity to complete an incomplete picture (Maier, 1994). This means that to be convincing, a scene need not be elaborately and completely decorated in order to create the desired illusion of place (Arnold, 1985). In the classroom, a couple of palm fronds are all that is needed to begin the illusion of a tropical ecosystem. Student's brains, with just a bit of the picture provided by scenery, can fill in the gaps and create a mental scene that enhances attention and engagement.

Costumes. As with scenery, just a bit of a costume goes a long way toward creating a more memorable experience. A Social Studies teacher could don a coonskin cap to increase attention as he provides insights into western expansion during the 1800's. And, there's nothing like a pair of lightning bolt earrings to complete the look for that first day of the electricity unit.

Music. In theater, the musical score serves to set the tone for the scene and to complement and punctuate the dramatic action onstage. The P.E. teacher who plays salsa music to keep the aerobic exercise going, and the writing instructor who plays soundtracks of softly chirping crickets behind the "summer nights" writing assignment both understand the value of an intentional musical treatment.

Special Effects. Special effects serve to add interest, surprise, and focus to the learning tasks at hand. A Chemistry teacher freezes rubber balls in liquid Nitrogen and then shatters them for effect. A literature teacher plays high pitched whale sounds as she introduces *Moby Dick* (Melville, 1851). A middle school teacher turns out the classroom lights and uses a flashlight to up-light her face as she reads from Edgar Allen Poe's *The Raven*. "Once upon a midnight dreary, while I pondered weak and weary…" (Poe, 1845).

ELABORATIONS AND EXTRA NOTES

examples, applicatons, implications, connections, questions, adjustments, deeper layers, reactions, times not to ...

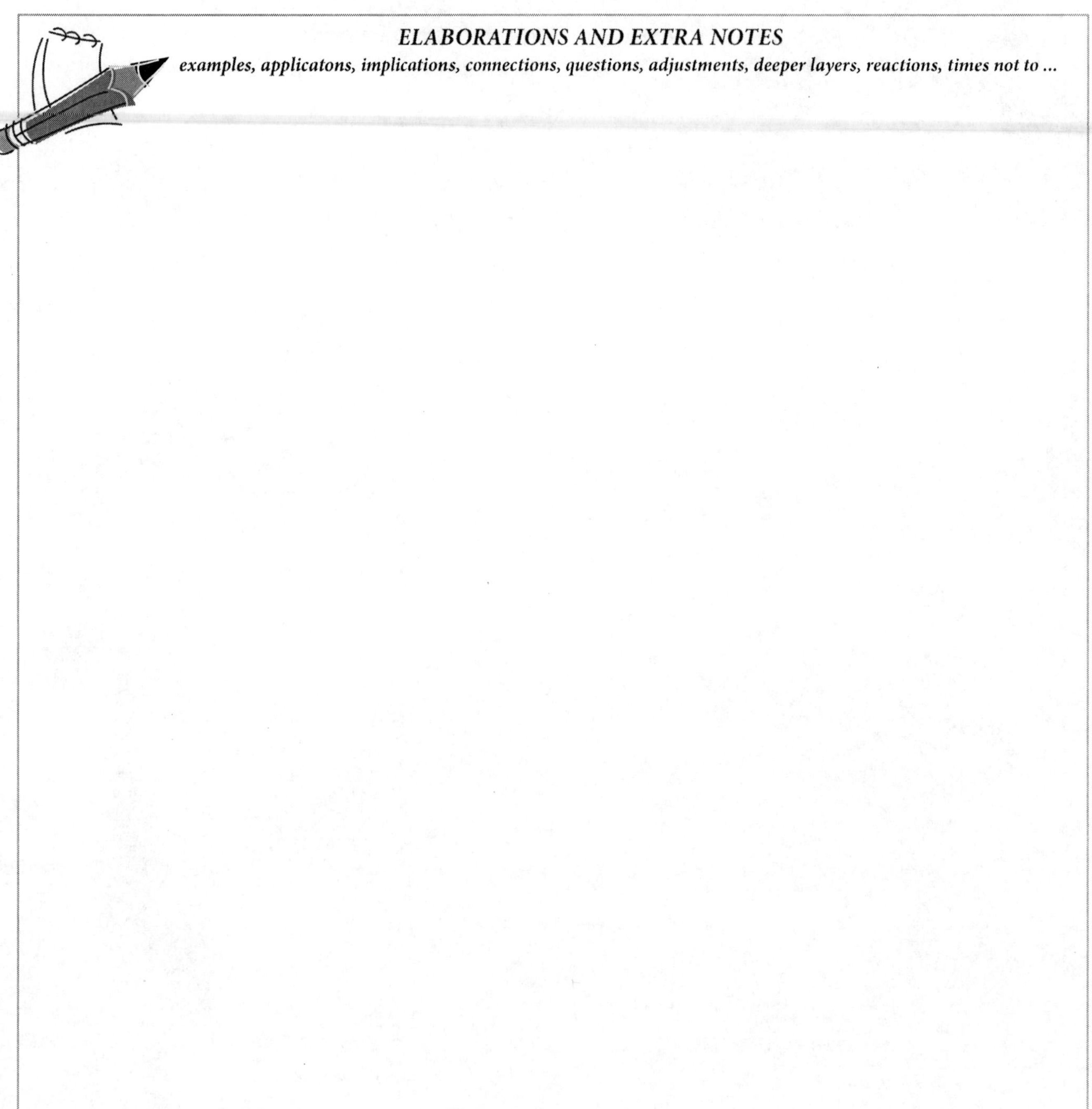
ELABORATIONS AND EXTRA NOTES
examples, applicatons, implications, connections, questions, adjustments, deeper layers, reactions, times not to ...

THEME **20**

Complementary Elements

Complementary Elements

Definition. The ability of the teacher to sequence instructional experiences that build on the preceding and set the stage for the subsequent.

Elaboration. A well-designed sequence of classroom experiences (usually a pair, occasionally three) can produce a more elaborate learning experience in total, than each of the parts can contribute individually. It seems, with just the right set-up or follow-up, 1 + 1 can = 3. Apple pie is good and vanilla ice cream is too. But together they are "apple pie a-la-mode." Good + good = great!

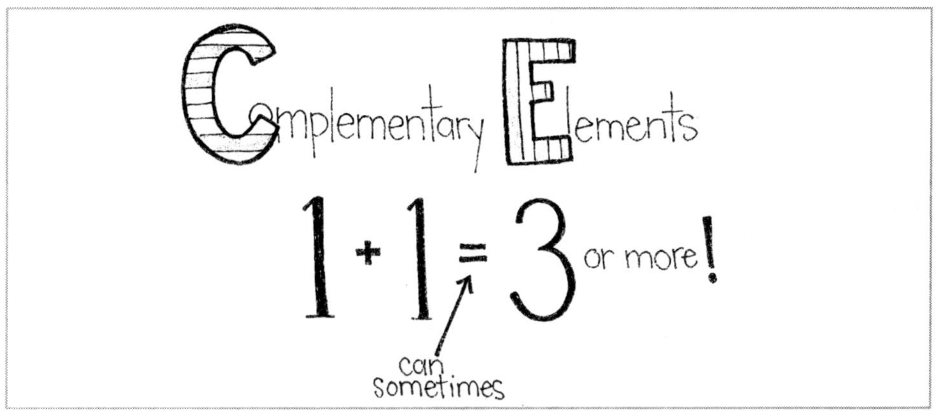

Think twice before you speak, because your words and influence will plant the seed of either success or failure in the mind of another.

– Napoleon Hill

Real knowledge is to know the extent of one's ignorance.

- Confucius

Two things can be said to be complementary when they, in a way of thinking, complete each other. The Free Dictionary.com defines complementary as *"combining two or more things in such a way as to enhance or emphasize each thing's qualities."* Merriam Webster's Collegiate Dictionary (10th Edition) offers *"Serving to fill out or complete"* and *"mutually supplying each other's lack."*

Complementary colors can make a room's paint scheme "come together." A well chosen tie or scarf can complete an outfit in a stylish way. In both cases, the elements were entirely satisfactory when considered individually, but when taken together, were enhanced. The total effect becomes greater than the sum of the parts.

In the culinary arts, a chef creates a series of courses that fit perfectly in sequence…a tart salad followed by a savory second course, followed by a sweet dessert. Each course is delicious individually, but when enjoyed in sequence, the effect is much enhanced. Some food parings are so classically complementary that we are used to seeing them together, like a hotdog with chili, peanut butter and jelly, cookies and milk, French fries and ketchup, or wine and cheese (Page & Dornenberg, 2008).

In music composition, a composer creates an opening movement that slowly builds momentum, then follows with virtuoso performances on individual instruments, then allows for a time of disharmony, which is, at the perfect time, then reconciled into a triumphant chorus. Each movement is made more impactful by positioning it next to another movement that is different, yet complementary (Arnold, 1985; Belkin, 2008).

In the classroom, just like in the kitchen or concert hall, learning can be greatly enhanced by positioning individual instructional episodes next to complementary ones. A 3rd grade teacher begins the day with an individual reflective time of journaling, then transitions into a whole group movement oriented activity, then to a small group, cooperative learning session, then back to an individual time of elaboration and question generation, then to a whole group Q/A game, then a short break, then some more... just like a fine meal proceeds from course to course, the preceding sets the stage for the subsequent. The total effect is greater than the sum of the parts.

While there is not a precise formula for designing classroom elements that are complementary, there are classical patterns or "types" of complementary elements that teachers can use to design complementary elements.

Completeness. In the movie Jerry Maguire (TriStar Pictures, 1996), Tom Cruise speaks the memorable romantic line *"I love you... you complete me."* to Renee Zellweger. When two elements complete each other, one element contains aspects that are lacking in the other. The two elements, taken together, form a whole. Presumably, Tom Cruise's character, Jerry, recognized that Renee Zellweger's character, Dorothy, possessed character or personality traits that he did not. Evidently, she agreed. Her response, perhaps even more memorable, was *"Shut up, just shut up. You had me at hello."*

Likewise a teacher might position a free writing time, where students write quickly and unhindered by convention, next to a proofing activity, where students identify and correct grammar and usage errors in their and other's free writing work. One learning experience completes the other.

Yin-Yang. According to ancient Chinese philosophy, the concept of yin and yang represents a balance between the universe's opposing, yet complementary forces. Yin-yang complements are dependent on one another for their very existence. Yin Yang literally means dark and light. The concept of darkness is meaningless without an understanding of light. Masculine is undefined without

...just like a fine meal proceeds from course to course, the preceding sets the stage for the subsequent. The total effect is greater than the sum of the parts.

And what, Socrates, is the food of the soul? Surely, I said, knowledge is the food of the soul.

– Plato

an understanding of feminine. To recognize good, one must acknowledge the absence of good, or evil (Latener & Leon, 2005, p. 869).

In the classroom, yin-yang complementary elements not only exist side by side in the instructional schedule for the day, but depend on each other to create comprehension. In acoustics, the teacher might position the concept of dissonant sound waves right next to the concept of resonant or harmonic waves. Comprehension of the one both precedes and requires comprehension of the other. Twist of plot, requires an understanding of predictable plot. Irony requires a prerequisite understanding of logic. The mathematical concept of zero is meaningless without the presence of a non-zero value. Adjectives don't exist without nouns, nor adverbs without verbs.

Contrast. This is perhaps the simplest and easiest to apply pattern of complementary elements. Contrast means that the complements are different from each other in some significant way. A fast paced, active session in the classroom can be followed by a lower energy, more reflective time. Collaborative work should be positioned adjacent to independent work. Difficult concepts are best positioned nearby easier concepts. Whole group instruction is best followed by activity centers or small group work. With the principle of contrast, it is not the case that there is just one best complement to any particular instructional element, but that the best complement to any instructional element is not more of the same element. Mashed potatoes are a great side dish to any number of entrees. But they don't go well with scalloped potatoes or baked potatoes. The best complement to a potato is a non-potato (Acheson, 2011).

Role Swap. The best follow-up to a session of question answering can be a session of question posing. Solving math problems is an excellent warm-up to designing and writing math problems. The learning produced by practicing a skill is deepened by a time of coaching and feedback to another's practice. The best way to learn something is to prepare to teach it to others. Speaking is developed through listening, and performances are enhanced by judging other performances.

Preliminary Practice. To provide students with preliminary practice means to isolate the harder parts of a skill and practice them separately before integrating the skills into a larger context. Especially for skills that require multiple steps or that employ a number of skills at once, it is effective to precede the skill work with a period of intense practice on the essential or most difficult skill (Hunter, 1982). For a set of word problems that require the addition of fractions with unlike denominators, the teacher might begin with a mini-lesson on finding the least common denominator. An orchestra teacher might ask students to practice a difficult measure of a performance prior to practicing the whole performance. An elementary math teacher does well to ask students to warm up by practicing writing vertical digits in a perfect column, before he introduces three digit subtraction. In all these cases, the complementary elements include a skill being taught right after the rehearsal of the skill's most difficult or essential component-a nice one-two punch.

The artist's world is limitless. It can be found anywhere, far from where he lives or a few feet away. It is always on his doorstep.

- Paul Strand

ELABORATIONS AND EXTRA NOTES
examples, applicatons, implications, connections, questions, adjustments, deeper layers, reactions, times not to ...

THEME 21

Time and Timing

Time and Timing

Definition. The ability of the teacher to appropriate the optimal amount of time to each instructional element, choose the most effective interval between elements of instruction, and utilize instructional elements at just the right place in the lesson to optimize their efficacy.

Elaboration. Timing is everything. The difference between an adequate experience and an excellent one is often found in the timing of the elements that comprise the experience, not so much in the elements themselves. This is particularly true of anything that is transactional in nature, where the essential action is found in the interplay of two people or combinations of individuals and groups.

Time is what we want most, but what we use worst.

– William Penn

Good timing is critical in stand-up comedy, public speaking, and storytelling. A successful auto salesman knows when to transition from shopping to buying (Oldroyd, McElheran, & Elkington, 2011). Musical composition is just as much about the spaces between the notes as the notes themselves (Goodridge, 1999). Effective parenting of teenagers requires one to choose the right time for sensitive discussions. Sports superstars do well to time their retirements with care, leaving

It is the timing of things, not only the things themselves, that leads to a successful outcome.

the sport just before they tarnish their legacy. In all these cases, something transactional is occurring between or among people. And, in all instances of human transaction, it is the timing of things, not only the things themselves, that leads to a successful outcome.

Teaching, of course, is highly transactional. Each school day is filled to the brim with human interaction. Teachers interact with students. Students interact with one another. Teachers and students interact with educational materials and technologies. In all these transactions, the difference between adequate outcomes and excellent outcomes is often the teacher's command of time and timing.

To better understand and apply the techniques of time and timing in the classroom, it is helpful to break the concept down into three component parts: *duration*, how long to do something; *interval*, how long to wait before doing the next thing; and, *readiness*, when to do something.

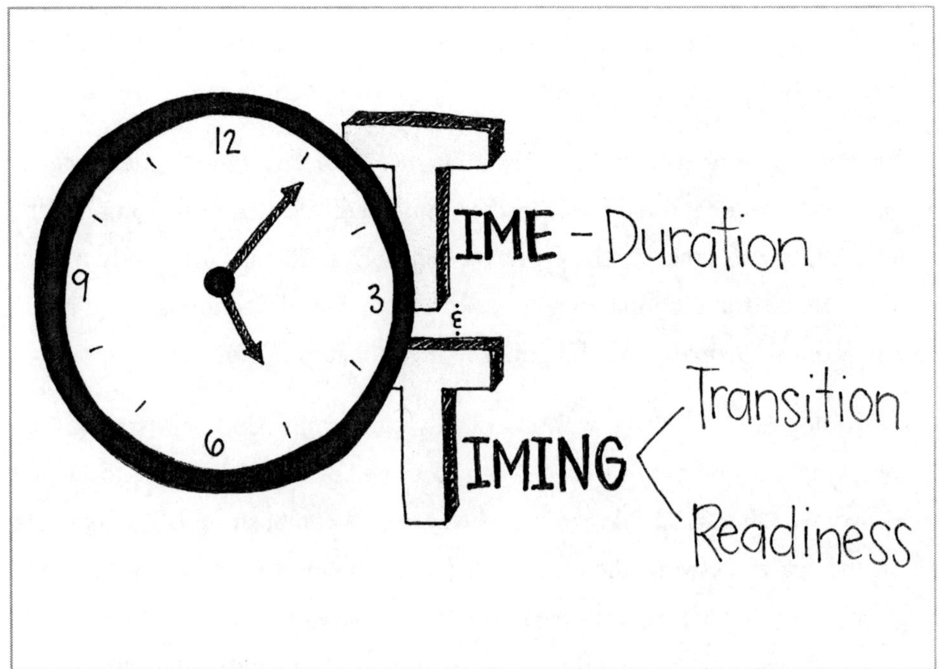

Duration. A comedian develops her "act" to last just under eight minutes. She designs three short pieces into the act at 45 seconds each, two longer pieces at ninety seconds each, and one ending piece that covers 2:45. She begins with a 45 second piece, then uses the two 90 second stories, then to another 45 second joke. She finishes with her best material after the audience is suitably warmed up-a brilliant 2:45 story with a wicked twist at the end. The audience screams for more but the comedian always leaves them wishing she would tell just one more joke ... she never does (Rutherford, 2009a, p. 2).

What is the optimal duration for an instructional device-a question, an experience, a written assignment, a discussion group, a hands-on activity, a cooperative learning structure, etc.? The optimal time is usually to end the device just ahead of the learner's dip in energy and interest, just like the comedian. All instructional devices have an energy curve over time. Typically, classroom activities start slow, build in energy and intensity, reach a maximum, and then begin to decline. An excellent time to end an activity is just before the maximum, not after. Why is this? There is a relationship among time, energy, and efficacy in every classroom (Matchock, 2010). When one episode of teaching ends just before the peak, the students can transfer the upward trend in energy to the next learning opportunity. This provides for a high energy closure for the preceding activity and a high energy beginning for the next one.

Interval. A well timed interval allows enough time for the audience (learners) to engage with the device- to complete a thought, to imagine an answer, to conjure a word-picture. The purpose of the interval is to clear the brain's working memory for the next set of items through a moment of transition (Rowe, 1974).

A rousing political speech has a flow to it. The key sound bites are surrounded by filler, transition, and water-treading. Too many nuggets delivered too often would overwhelm the listeners, too few would bore them. There is an optimal balance

O sweet, delusive Noon,
Which the morning
climbs to find,
O moment sped too soon,
And morning left behind.

- Helen Hunt Jackson

between nugget and filler and an optimal interval between each nugget. In stand-up comedy this perfect interval is called a comedic beat, just the right length of pause to set up the punch line.

In the well-timed classroom, transitions, wait time, segues, and pauses are designed to provide just enough time to extend thinking, but not enough to invite distraction (Smith, 1988). As a general guide, transitions between activities should be shorter when the activities are similar and longer when the activities are different (Atwood & Wilen, 1991). A longer transition is particularly helpful when the activities look similar but are not. Negative transfer and misconception abound when there is inadequate time between confusing concepts (Hunter, 1982). In a fine restaurant, the waiter will offer a palate cleanser, perhaps a bite of sorbet, between courses - a nice transition that prevents negative taste transfer.

Readiness. A successful salesperson doesn't go for the close when she is ready, but times the close to match the client's readiness. Likewise, a successful teacher looks for cues that the learners are ready for the next learning experience instead of simply following the pacing guide or lesson plan. Ten minutes of instruction delivered at a moment of peak readiness may be worth 100 minutes of instruction delivered at another time. Students can be ready *cognitively*, meaning that they are intellectually ready for the coming task. They can be ready *emotionally*, meaning that their affective state is a good fit for the type of learning to be experienced. They can be ready *experientially*, meaning that they have relevant and recent real-life experiences that can support and structure the new learning (Bredekamp & Shepard, 1990). Teachers should also consider students' *energy* readiness (Weith & Zacks, 2011). At 2:15 pm, after a morning field trip, a late lunch, and a big test, the students (and teacher) may be ready in every way other way, but there is just not enough energy available for success. "Let's start this tomorrow morning when we're fresh," the teacher says. It's all about timing.

The only reason for time is so that everything doesn't happen at once.
– Albert Einstein

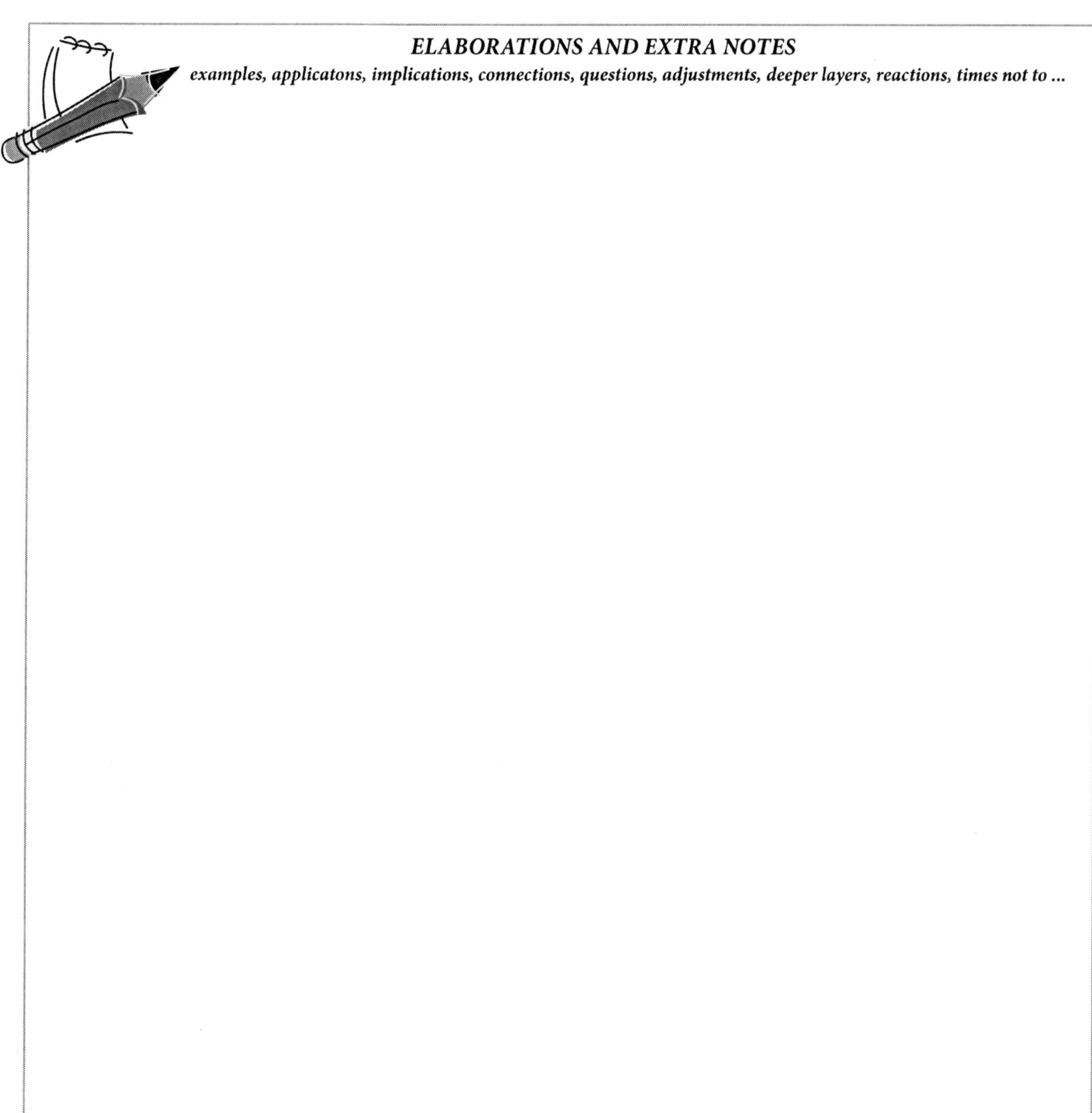

ELABORATIONS AND EXTRA NOTES
examples, applicatons, implications, connections, questions, adjustments, deeper layers, reactions, times not to ...

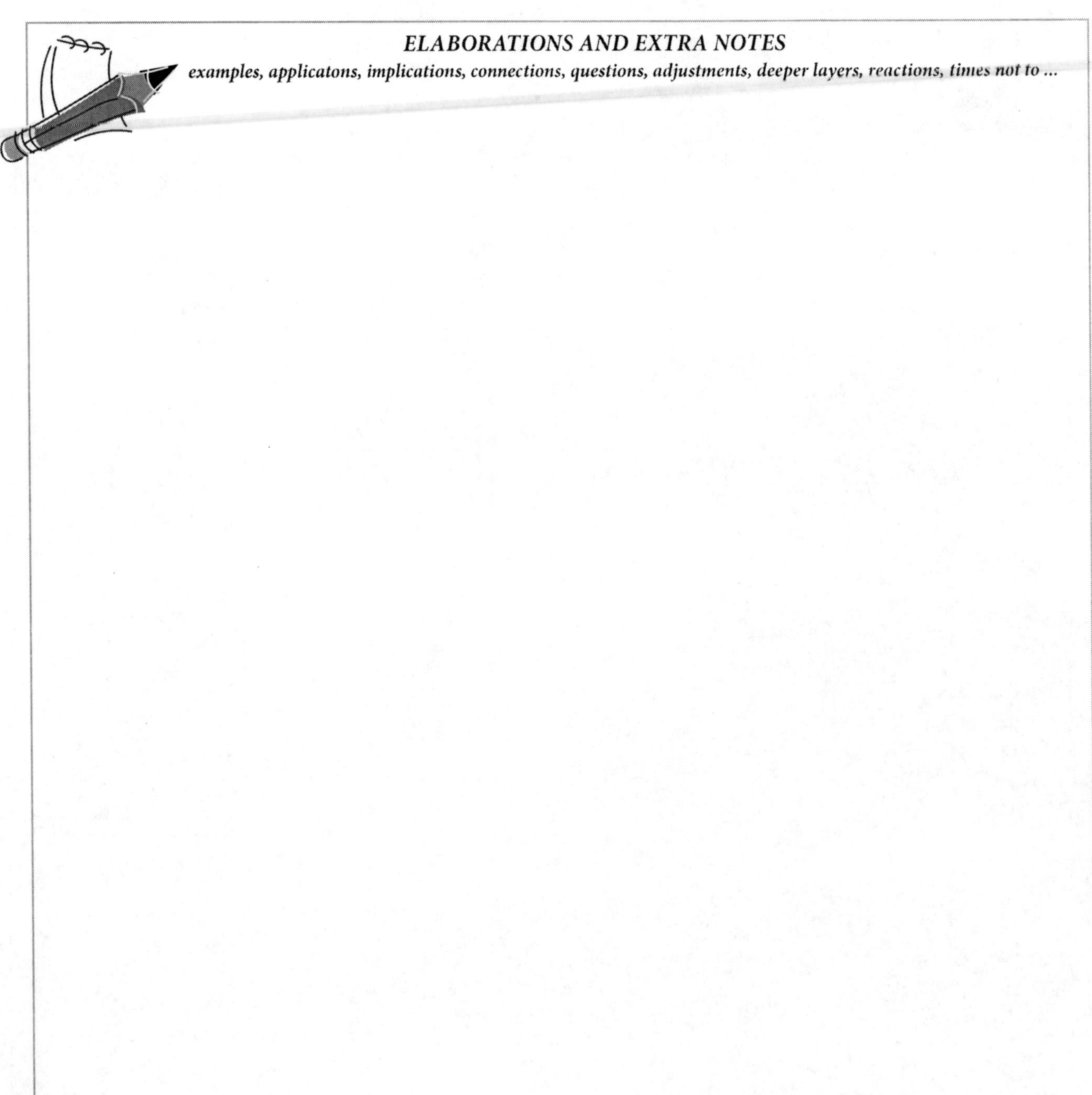
ELABORATIONS AND EXTRA NOTES
examples, applicatons, implications, connections, questions, adjustments, deeper layers, reactions, times not to ...

THEME 22A

PERSONAL PRESENCE

I've noticed that teachers who can't be described with a single word are more compelling than those who can be.

Personal Presence

Definition. The ability of the teacher to establish and maintain an interpersonal connection with students that is characterized by influence, affinity, interest, respect, admiration, loyalty, importance, efficacy, and positive regard.

Elaboration. Sometimes the reason a lesson is well-learned isn't the content of the lesson, the teacher's skill in planning and design, or the techniques used to present information or engage students. Sometimes, the reason for success is not primarily related to the lesson, but to the person who is teaching it. Call it respect, admiration, persona, credibility, influence, charisma, gravitas, or charm. By any name, it is the boost to learning that is bound up in the person of the teacher.

Much has been studied and written about the organizational effects of personal traits and characteristics. The leadership literature alone is substantial, not to mention contributions from the fields of psychology, personal development, and popular culture. Daniel Goleman in *Emotional Intelligence* points out that human emotions are contagious and humans appear to be designed to influence one another in powerful ways (Goleman, 1995). Stephen Covey in *Principal Centered Leadership* cites "thirty methods of influence." (1992, 119-128).

A leader is one who knows the way, goes the way, and shows the way.
– John C. Maxwell

An Army Captain asks for three volunteers from his platoon to accompany him in a dangerous rescue operation inside a small town in central Afghanistan. The captain, although barely older than the rest of the platoon members, commands much respect from his troops. During the previous three months he has proven himself to be not only a brave and disciplined soldier, but also a warm and approachable human. He is quick to admit his mistakes, first to offer encouragement, and slow to blame others. He leads through a quiet but strong, persuasive style. All twelve of the soldiers volunteer (Rutherford, 2009a, p. 3).

What are the attributes of leadership that combine to make this Army Captain so influential with his men? It seems to me that personal presence is easy to spot but difficult to define. Personal presence, unlike many of the other *Artisan Teacher* themes, is not so much a technique to be learned, but more a set of personal attributes that serve to draw others in and create relationships that support and enhance the work to be done. Still, based on many classroom observations, there are some patterns that emerge that can help teachers identify and develop traits that are important to their own personal presence.

Teacher traits and behaviors associated with personal presence.

Being present in the moment. Teachers have to do many things at once. They multi-task, deal with distractions, and try to balance work, home, and personal lives. Still, teachers are powerful when they are 100% present and available to the opportunity at hand - not thinking too far ahead, not dwelling in the past, not being preoccupied, not being self-focused. We all know what it's like to be in the presence of someone who is distracted. And, we've experienced how powerful a moment can be when the person we're sharing it with is "all-in" with us (Bowling & Hoffman, 2000). With all distractions and pressures of the classroom swirling around in a teacher's mind… those that can, if just for a moment, block it all out and simply be present and available to students are exercising a powerful component of personal presence.

A little personal complexity. I've noticed that teachers who can't be described with a single word are more compelling to students than those who can be. "He's strict, but spontaneous." This is not to suggest that teachers should be complicated and unpredictable. It is just an observation based on many, many classroom visits. A little complexity draws students' attention and engagement. It makes the teacher more unique, more interesting, and more memorable (Leiter & Maslach, 2006).

Princess Diana is greatly loved and admired throughout the world. Perhaps her most endearing characteristic was her ability to be, at once, royal and common. She was Diana, Princess of Wales, a member of the British Royal Family, and also a former kindergarten teacher… both. This duality is often a part of strong personal presence. We are drawn to individuals who are intelligent - yet approachable, beautiful - yet humble, large - yet gentle, silly - yet profound, or accomplished - yet other-focused.

Art doesn't transform. It just plain forms.
– Roy Lichtenstein

When I think of art I think of beauty. Beauty is the mystery of life. It is not in the eye it is in the mind. In our minds there is awareness of perfection.

– Agnes Martin

Being influence-able. Students are more influenced by teachers who are influenced by their students. Influence, like trust and communication, is a two-way street (Fukushima, 1999). A teacher might say to students "I've changed my thinking after reading your paper. You've convinced me that…" or "I was a little down this morning and not in the best of moods. But, after working with you guys for just a few minutes on this and seeing your good ideas, I feel a lot better. Thank you for that!" These words signal that what students do personally affects the thoughts and feelings of the teacher. Interesting isn't it… being *influence-able* makes the teacher more *influential.*

Loss of self-consciousness. There is something extra compelling about a teacher that occasionally becomes so engaged in the lesson that they temporarily forget to worry about what others think of them. I suspect this is because students are themselves self-conscious beings and to see another person (the teacher) temporarily freed from the normal state of "worrying what others think" is compelling indeed.

I vividly remember watching my 11th grade chemistry teacher, Everett Smith, lead us through an experiment. He became giddy with excitement and anticipation waiting for the reaction to occur! We all made fun of Mr. Smith for being "so into it," but privately, I envied him. I remember thinking to myself "One day I hope I have a job that I enjoy as much as Mr. Smith enjoys teaching chemistry." By the way, five years later, I became a chemistry teacher myself - in no small part because of Mr. Smith's personal presence.

Mihaly Csikszentmihalyi (1990), in his national best-seller *FLOW- The Psychology of Optimal Experience*, identifies loss of self-consciousness as a key indicator of the Flow state (pp. 62-63). Flow, according to Csikszentmihalyi, is the state of being completely caught up in an activity such that it is enjoyable and satisfying. A violinist, in the middle of a concert, or a rock climber, completing a technically difficult part of an ascent might be said to be in a state of flow. Csikszentmihalyi concludes loss of self-consciousness is often accompanied by a sense that time does not pass in the way in usually does. "It can't be 2:30 yet, that's not possible. It seems we just got stated."

Give whatever you are doing and whoever you are with the gift of your attention.

– Jim Rohn

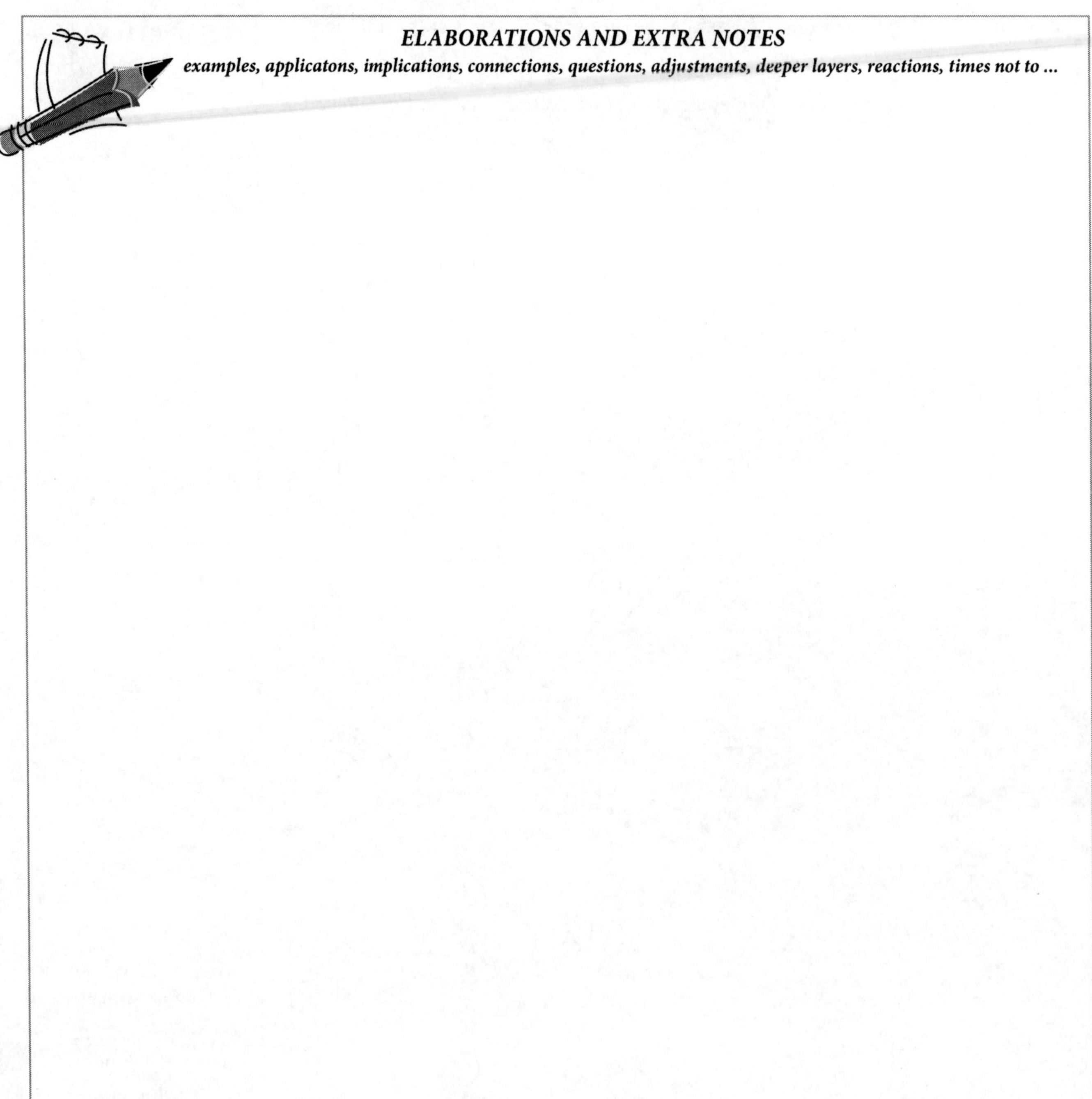
ELABORATIONS AND EXTRA NOTES
examples, applicatons, implications, connections, questions, adjustments, deeper layers, reactions, times not to ...

THEME 23 Delight

FIELD NOTES:

Delights, being surprises, create strong memories.

Delight

Definition. The ability of the teacher to create instances of learning that are particularly pleasing, charming, unexpected, or surprising… to create a moment that is unforgettable, has a twist, or exceeds expectations.

Elaboration. A delight is a positive surprise. When something happens that benefits us and we were not expecting it to happen, we experience the sensation of delight. We usually respond to a delight with an exclamation of "oh my" or "wow", or at least a broad smile. Recently I pulled on a pair of old jeans that I had not worn in quite a while. I was delighted to find a crumpled five dollar bill in the pocket… "sweet!" I said to myself. The essence of delight is surprise.

Surprise enhances memory (Fletcher, Anderson, Shanks, Honey, Carpenter, Donovan, Papadakis & Bullmore, 2001). The human brain is oriented toward survival. We like crossword puzzles, music, and stimulating conversations, but the primary function of our brain, from an evolutionary perspective, is the survival of our physical bodies in the current environment (Schoen, 2013). One of the ways the brain works for our survival is to predict the near future. When the

brain successfully predicts what will happen next, we are prepared for it and this increases our chances of surviving it. So, in an operational sense, the brain does not like surprises. A surprise is a failure to predict the immediate future. As such, the brain pays especially close attention to surprises, so as to not be fooled again. If a disembodied brain could talk, it might say, after encountering a surprise, "Fool me once, shame on you. Fool me twice, shame on me."

For the record, negative surprises enhance recall too (D'Argembeau, Comblain & Ven der Linden, 2002). I remember gathering some firewood from a stack one day and uncovering a snake coiled up between the logs. Fortunately it was cold outside and the snake didn't move. Still, from that moment on, every time I approach a stack of firewood, my brain instantly recalls the image of the coiled snake. Since they are linked to our survival, surprises are extra-memorable. We are designed to remember well things that surprise us.

Happiness often sneaks in through a door you didn't know you left open.

– John Barrymore

When we survive an occurrence that was not predicted, we experience a moment of relief that the occurrence didn't do us in. "Whew, that was a close one." When the occurrence turns out to be pleasant, and not just a near miss of something unpleasant, we experience an acute double sensation. We find ourselves not only surviving an unpredicted occurrence, but benefiting from it as well. This sense of "Whew" plus "Oh my" is one way of understanding the sensation of delight.

Delights, being surprises, create strong memories. These "delight memories" can serve as navigation aids (signposts, waypoints, memory markers) in a student's memory. This allows faster and truer navigation back to the memory when recall is initiated (Fletcher, et al. 2001).

Types of delight.

Random act of positivity delight. We tend to remember extraordinarily positive events (D'Archembeau, et al. 2002). I was in the drive-through lane at a fast food restaurant a few days before Christmas one year. When I reached the window, the young server said "The car ahead of you paid for your food. He said to tell you Merry Christmas." I'll never forget that.

A fourth grade teacher was working individually with a struggling student on converting fractions to decimals. After the student got a few problems in a row just right, the teacher said "Wow, Carl, you've got it now, good work." Carl said, "Yeah, I think your calculator is lucky for me. I was getting them all wrong on mine." The teacher took a sharpie pen and wrote Carl's name on the back of her calculator and gave it to him. "Don't tell anyone I gave you this," she said. "Whenever you use it, remember how you learned to convert fractions to decimals on it." "Wow, thanks." said Carl as he grinned from ear to ear.

Suspense-resolution delight. We tend to remember how things begin and end (Sousa, 1995). The seventh-grade math teacher placed a huge glass jar of jelly

Some cause happiness wherever they go; others whenever they go.
- Oscar Wilde

The mere imparting of information is not education.
– Carter G. Woodson

beans on the front table. Students, as part of their probability and estimation unit, were asked to examine the jar all week and be ready to estimate the number of jelly beans on Friday. Throughout the week, the teacher introduced various ways to estimate the total - by volume, by weight, by appearance, and so on. On Friday the teacher asked the students to play a drum roll on their desks before revealing the true number of jelly beans… 1,458! Three months later, while reviewing for end of year exams, the teacher asked "How many of you remember the jar of jelly beans and the ways we estimated their number?" Every hand was raised.

Preparation delight. The 11th graders were expecting a typical day of teaching and learning in Mrs. Sullivan's Business Education class Wednesday afternoon. They were surprised and amazed at the scene as they entered the room. The tables were set with linen and fine china, flowers were at each table, classical music played in the background, and each student's name was carefully engraved on place cards. "Ooohs and Ahhhs" filled the classroom as students entered to begin their unit on business etiquette. Ten years later, at an important business diner with key clients, Marion still remembers that day as she confidently selects the shrimp fork for the next course.

Twist of plot delight. We remember times that we were fooled (Schoen, 2013). A writer weaves an interesting and entertaining plot, then delivers a delightful twist at the end taking the story in a completely unexpected direction. The reader immediately re-reads the chapter and smiles.

The fifth graders were seated on the carpet, ready to listen in as their teacher read a few key passages from *Tears of a Tiger*, by Sharon M. Draper, one of their favorite authors. In addition to enjoying the story, the students were working on understanding how the author's purpose influences a piece of writing. The teacher reads a few paragraphs and stops. "Wouldn't it be great if we could really ask the author what her purpose was in writing this book?" "What do you think she would say?" At that moment, Sharon Draper walks out from behind a curtain and says to the class, "Well, let's talk about that." Unbeknown to the class, Sharon Draper and the teacher were sorority sisters in college. Sharon often drops in to surprise students and answer their questions. They will never forget that day's discussion of author's purpose.

Exceeds expectations delight. We remember when things turn out better than we thought they would (D'Archembeau, et al. 2002). A business traveler enters the department store at 8:55 pm looking for a clean shirt to wear the next day. "How late do you stay open?" he asks the salesperson. "As long as you need us," the salesperson replies. As the traveler hurries to make his purchase he thinks how unexpected that response was and how he'll remember to shop here more often (Rutherford, 2009, p. 4).

Jasmine, a 2nd grader, had been absent for two days. The note from the office said that she had the flu. On the evening of the second day, Jasmine's teacher called her home to check on her, ask if there was anything she needed from school, and just to express to Jasmine's mother how she and the class missed Jasmine and hoped she would return soon. The young mother was delighted at the call. "It was more than I expected" she said to at least a dozen other parents over the next two weeks.

Design delight. It is memorable whenever we encounter something that is particularly well made or well designed for its purpose. A great design often catches us by surprise and we remember our first experience with it (Fletcher, et al. 2001).

A new car model has designed all the key controls for audio, navigation, and climate control into the steering wheel, just inches from the driver's fingertips. As the driver changes radio stations while keeping her eyes on the road she thinks how cool that is… a grin appears on her face.

All claims of education notwithstanding, the pupil will accept only that which his mind craves.

– Emma Goldman

The key to education is the experience of beauty.
– Friedrich Schiller

Fourth graders are examining a multiplication table that arranges factors and products as a grid. The teacher shows them how they can use the table to check their multiplication facts up thorough 12 x 12 = 144. "Not bad" the students say as they get accustomed to using the table. Then, the teacher shows them how they can place two fingers on any two numbers that are vertically adjacent and trace a line straight back to the left side of the table to show any fraction's simplified form. "Wow, said one student. Can I take this home?"

ELABORATIONS AND EXTRA NOTES

examples, applicatons, implications, connections, questions, adjustments, deeper layers, reactions, times not to ...

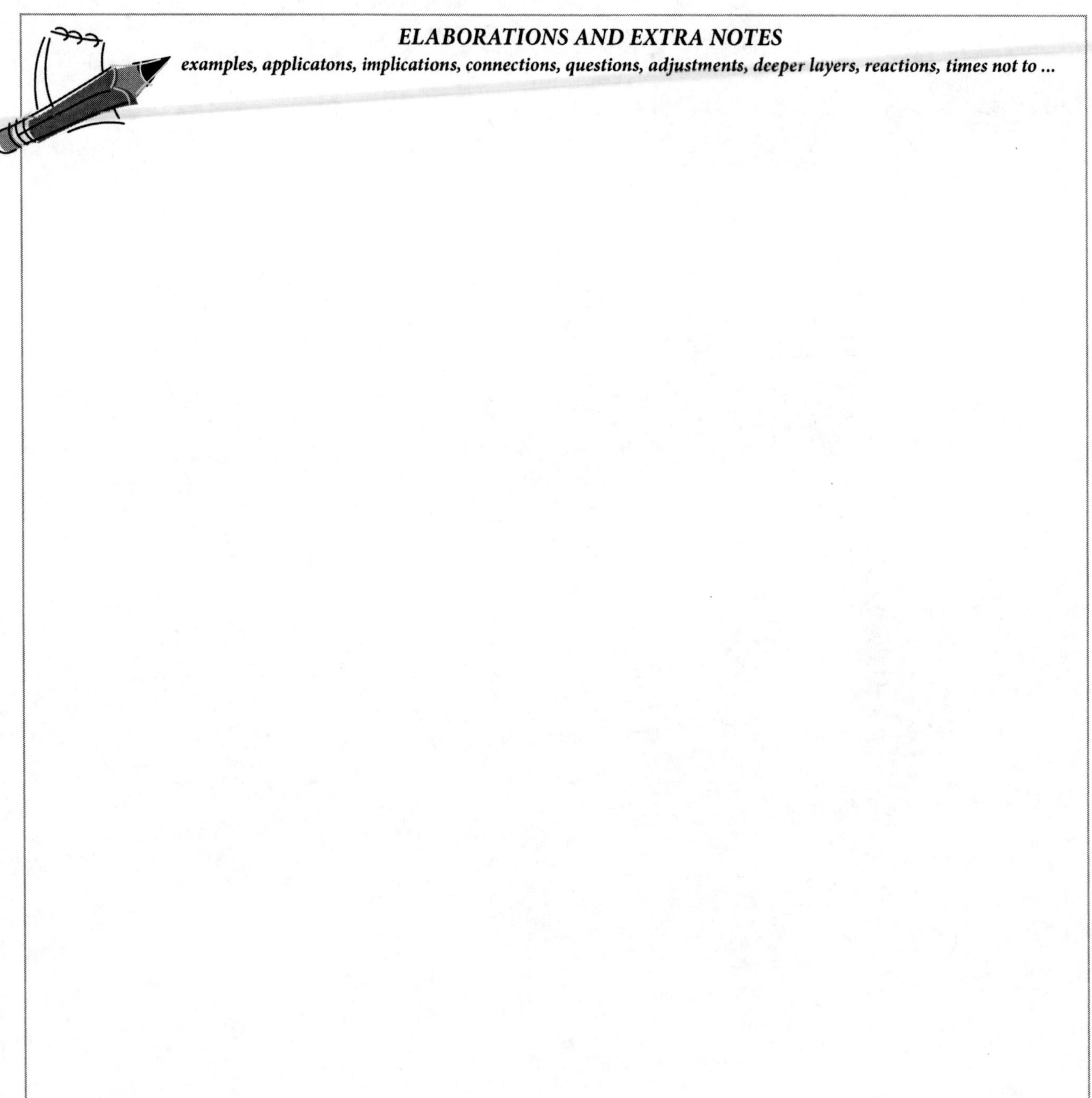

ELABORATIONS AND EXTRA NOTES

examples, applicatons, implications, connections, questions, adjustments, deeper layers, reactions, times not to ...

End Notes 

I once had the opportunity to participate in a leadership development experience that paired schools and businesses for the purpose of sharing ideas and strategies for success. The business partner I worked with was Hixson Architecture, Engineering, and Interiors in Cincinnati, Ohio. After a quick tour of the facilities, I sat down with Hixson CEO Wick Ach and asked him what leadership insights he might share that I could apply to education. His answer was surprising and memorable.

He walked over to the whiteboard and wrote four large letters- GPTW. He then tossed the marker back into the tray and sat down at this desk. "That's it" he said. "That's my strategy." He went on to explain that GPTW stood for Great Place To Work. Back at the whiteboard now, Mr. Ach drew a series of connected arrows like a flow chart. He explained "My job as CEO is to make Hixson a great place to work. If I do that well, (he drew an arrow from GPTW to the words 'best architects and engineers') I'll attract and keep the best architects and engineers. Over time, those architects and engineers will create satisfied clients (He connected 'best architects and engineers to the words 'satisfied clients'). Satisfied clients come back for repeat business. Repeat business drives our profitability (He finished with arrows to repeat business and then profitability). It's that simple," he said, "and it all starts with creating a GPTW."

He finished by saying "I'm not an education expert. But, if I was a school principal, I'd take the same approach. In fact" he said, "I'd draw it up just like this except I'd swap *great teachers* for *great architects and engineers* and I'd swap *student learning* for *profitability*. Everything else would stay the same."

I agree wholeheartedly. In fact, as I reflect on the thousands of observations and school visits that provide the basis for the *Artisan Teacher Field Guide*, I think I can now take the GPTW approach a step further and describe some characteristics of schools that attract and keep great teachers—*Artisan Teachers.*

Over time, some schools attract and retain more than their fair share of artisan teachers while other schools lose their most talented teachers. I've found that great teachers are not necessarily like athletic free agents, willing to go anywhere to play for the highest bidder. I have noticed, however, that they will drive past several schools closer to their home to find a place that suits their needs. What are they looking for? What school characteristics turn out to be most inviting for highly talented, artisan teachers?

Artisan Teachers Work Where They Are *Valued*.

What teacher characteristics are valued most at your school? Is it a teacher's good attitude, work ethic, local community connections, years of experience, or extracurricular activities? All these attributes are valuable, of course. A GPTW values teachers' instructional talents and skills above everything else.

Artisan Teachers Work Where They Are *Appreciated*.

One definition of appreciate is *"to be fully conscious of, to be aware of, to detect"* (dictionary.com), as in a person who appreciates modern art or fine wine. I believe talented teachers seek out settings where administrators know what great teaching looks like and understand the finer points and nuances of effective teaching.

Artisan Teachers Work Where They Are *Recognized*.

In artisan-friendly schools administrators regularly point out effective episodes of instruction. They provide immediate and specific feedback to teachers on their instructional moves and strategies. The key is to provide abundant, immediate, and specific recognition of teachers' talents, not in a general way as in "*nice job*," but specifically as in *"when you..., that caused..."*

Artisan Teachers Work Where They Can Be *Developed*.

Ultimately, the greatest attractor of artisanship is the opportunity for growth and development. Some administrators focus much of their classroom observation time on evaluation instruments or supervisory walkthroughs. Administrators in artisan-friendly schools focus their energies mostly on the development of teachers and teaching. They agree with that old Iowa proverb, *"You don't make the lambs fatter by weighing them more often. You make them fatter by feeding them."* Administrators who develop a reputation for developing artisanship will, over time, attract more than their fair share of it (Rutherford, 2010).

It is my sincere wish that the descriptions and illustrations of teacher artisanship contained in *The Artisan Teacher: A Field Guide to Skillful Teaching* will serve as a valuable, trustworthy, and easy to use resource for creating and sustaining a Great Place to Work.

References

Acheson, H. (2011). *A new turn in the south: Southern flavors reinvented for your kitchen.* New York: Crown Publishing Group.

Alexander, C., Ishakawa, S., Fiksdahl-King, I., & Shlomo, S. (1977). *A pattern language: towns, buildings, construction.* Berkely, CA: Center for Environmental Structure.

Ali, R.J., Kor, L.K. (2007). Association between brain hemisphericity, learning styles, and confidence in using graphics calculator for mathematics. *Eurasia Journal of Mathematics, Science, and Technology, 3*(2), 127-131.

Arcavi, A. (1994). Symbol sense: Informal sense making in formal mathematics. *For the Learning of Mathematics, 14*(3), 24-35.

Arlin, M. (1984). Time, Equality, and Mastery Learning. *Review of Educational Research, 54*(1), 65-86.

Arnold, R.L. (1985). *Scene technology.* Delran, NJ: Simon & Schuster.

Ashcraft, M. (1994). *Human memory and cognition.* New York, New York: HarperCollins.

Atkinson, R. and Shifflin, R. (1971). The control of short term memory. *Scientific American, 224*, 82-90.

Atwood, V.A. & Wilen, W.W. (1991). Wait time and effective Social Studies instruction: What can research in science education tell us? *Social Education, 55*, 179-181.

Awh, E., Jonides, J. & Reuter-Lorenz, P. (1998). Rehearsal in spatial working memory. *Journal of Experimental Psychology: Human Perception and Performance, 24*(3), 780-790.

Baddeley, A. (1986). *Working memory.* Oxford, England: Clarendon Press.

Baker, K.R. (1974). *Introduction to sequencing and scheduling.* New York, NY: Jon Wiley and Sons.

Barner, D., Thalwitz, D., Wood, J., Yang, S.J., & Carey, S., (2007). On the relation between the acquisition of singular-plural morpho-syntax and the concxeptual distinction between one and more than one. *Developmental Science, 10*(3), 365-373.

Bartlett, F.C. (1932). *Remembering: A study in experimental and social psychology.* Cambridge, England: Cambridge University Press.

Bateson, P. (2003). The promise of behavioural biology. *Animal Behavior, 65*, 11-17.

Belkin, A. (2008). A practical guide to musical composition. (e-book in PDF format from www.webdepot.umontreal.ca.)

Bhattacharya, K., & Han, S. (2001). Piaget and cognitive development. In M. Orey (Ed.), *Emerging perspectives on learning, teaching, and technology.* Retrieved 1/6/13, from http://projects.coe.uga.edu/epltt/.

Bjork, R.A. & Richardson-Klavhen, A. (1989). On the puzzling relationship between environmental context and human memory. *Current Issues in Cognitive Processes.* Hillsdale, NJ: Earlbaum.

Black, P. & William, D. (1998). Inside the black box: Raising standards through classroom assessment. *Phi Delta Kappan, 80*, 139-144.

Bloom, B. (1956). *Taxonomy of educational objectives: The classification of educational goals, Handbook I: Cognitive Domain.* New York, NY: Longman.

Bowling, D. & Hoffman, D. (2000). Bringing peace into the room: The personal qualities of the mediator and their impact on the mediation. *Negotiation Journal, 16*, 5-28.

Boyle, J.R., & Weishaar, M. (1997). The effects of expert-generated versus student-generated cognitive organizers on the reading comprehension of students with learning disabilities. *Learning Disabilities Research an Practice, 12*(4), 228-235.

Bransford, J. D., Brown, A. L., & Cocking, R. (2000). *How people learn: brain, mind, experience, and school.* Washington, DC: National Academy Press.

Bransford, J. D., Brown, A. L., & Cocking, R. (2000). *How people learn: Brain, mind, experience, and school.* Washington, DC: National Academy Press.

Bredekamp, S. & Shepard, L. (1990). *Reaching potentials: appropriate curriculum and assessmen for young children.* Washington, D.C.: National Association for the Education of Young Children.

Brophy, J. (1987). Synthesis of research on strategies for motivating students to learn. *Educational Leadership, 45*(2), 40-48.

Cahill, L., Gorski, L., & Le, K. (2003). Enhanced human memory consolidation with post-learning stress: Interaction with the degree of arousal at encoding. *Learning & Memory, 10*, 270-274.

Caine, R. N. & Caine, G.(1994). *Making connections: Teaching and the human brain.* Alexandria, VA: Association for Supervision and Curriculum Development.

Carroll, J.B. (1963). A Model of School Learning. *Teachers College Record, 64*, 723-733.

Ciofalo, J.F. & Wylie, E.C. (2006). Using diagnostic classroom assessment: One question at a time. *Teachers College Record*, Date published: January 10, 2006. http://www.tcrecord.org/Home.asp ID Number: 12285, Date Accessed: 12/30/12.

Cohen, N.J. & Eichenbaum, H. (1993). *Memory, amnesia, and the hippocampal system.* Cambridge, MA: MIT Press.

Coleridge, S.T. (1817). *Biographia litteraria.* London, England: S. Curtis, Printer. (digitized by Google).

Cory, G. & Gardner, R. (2002). *The evolutionary neuroethology of Paul MacLean.* Westport, CT: Praeger Publishers.

Covey, S. (1989). *The 7 habits of highly effective people.* New York, NY: Free Press.

Covey, S. (1992). *Principle centered leadership.* New York, NY: Free Press.

Cowan, N. (1997). *Attention and memory an integrated framework.* New York: Oxford University Press.

Csikszentmihalyi, M. (1990). *Flow: The psychology of optimal experience.* New York, NY: HarperCollins.

Cummings, C. (1992). *Managing to teach.* Edmonds, WA: Teaching Inc.

D'Archembeau, A., Comblain, C., & Van der Linden, M. (2002). Phenomenal characteristics of autobiographical memories for positive, negative, and neutral events. *Applied Cognitive Psychology, 17*(3), 281-294.

Damasio, A. (1994). *Descartes' error: Emotion, reason, and the human brain.* New York, NY: G.P. Putnam & Sons.

Diamond, M. (1984). *Enriching heredity.* New York, New York: Free Press.

Diamond, M., Johnson, R., & Ingham, C. (1971). Brain plasticity induced by environment and pregnancy. *Neuroscience, 2*, 171-178.

Doyle, A.C. (1930). *A study in scarlet, The complete Sherlock Holmes.* New York, NY: Doubleday.

Dunn, J. L., Alderfer, J., & Lehman, P. (2001). *National Geographic field guide to the birds of eastern North America.* Washington, DC: National Geographic Press.

Dwyer, C. (2008). *The future of assessment: Shaping teaching and learning.* New York, NY: Erlbaum.

Ericsson, K. (2007). Deliberate practice and the modifiability of body and mind: Toward a science of the structure and acquisition of expert and elite performance. *International Journal of Sport Psychology, 38*, 4-34.

Ericsson, K. (2009). Toward a science of exceptional achievement: Attaining superior performance through deliberate practice. *Annals of New York Academy of Science, 1172*, 199-217.

Feather, N.T. (1982). *Expectancy-value approaches: Present status and future diections.* In Feather, N.T. (ed.), Expectations and actions: Expectancy-value models in psychology. Hillsdale, NJ: Erlbaum.

Feather, N.T. (1992). Values, valences, expectations, and actions. *Journal of Social Issues, 48*, 109-124.

Fieldbook for boys and men. (1967). Boy Scouts of America. Garden City, NY: Doubleday.

Fletcher, P.C., Anderson, J.M., Shanks, D.R., Honey, R., Carpenter, T.A., Donovan, T., Papadakis, N., & Bullmore, E.T. (2001). Responses of human frontal cortex to surprising events are predicted by formal associative learning theory. *Nature Neuroscience, 4*(10), 1043-1048.

Fukushima, S. (1999). What you bring to the table: Transference and countertransference in the negotiation process. *Negotiation Journal, 15*, 169.

Gagne, R.M. (1963). Military training and the principles of learning. *American Psychologist*, 83-91.

Gagne, R.M., Briggs, L.J., & Wagner, W.W. (1992). *The principles of instructional design.* Ft.Worth, TX: Harcourt Brace Jovanovich College Publishers.

Gardner, H. (1983). *Frames of mind: The theory of multiple intelligences.* New York, NY: Basic Books.

Gardner, H. and Hatch, T. (1989). Multiple intelligences go to school: Educational implications of the theory of multiple intelligences. *Educational Researcher, 18*(8), 4-9.

Garrison, C., & Ehringhaus, M. (2007). Formative and summative assessments in the classroom. Retrieved from http://www.amle.org/Publications/WebExclusive/Assessment/tabid/1120/Default.aspx.

Ghazanfar, A., & Schroeder, C.E. (2006). Is neocortex essentially multisensory? *Trends in Cognitive Science, 10*, 278-285.

Goldberg, F.M., & McDermott, L.C., (1987). An investigation of student understanding of the real image formed by a converging lens or concave mirror, *American Journal of Physics, 55*(2), 108-120.

Goleman, D. (1995). *Emotional intelligence: Why it can matter more than IQ*. New York, NY: Bantam Books.

Goodridge, J. (1999). *Rhythm and timing of movement in performance: Drama, dance and ceremony.* London, U.K.: Jessica Kingsley Publishers.

Grainer, R. (2010). *Suspending disbelief: Theater as a context for sharing.* Sussex, UK: Sussex Academic Press.

Gutierrez, R. & Slavin, R. (1991). *Achievement effects of the non-graded elementary school: A retrospective review.* Baltimore, MD: Johns Hopkins University.

Hart, L. (1983). *Human brain and human learning.* White Plains, NY: Longman.

Hattie, J., & Timperley, H. (2007). The power of feedback. *Review of Educational Research, 77*, 81-112.

Hebb, D.O. (1949). *The organization of behavior.* New York, NY: John Wiley & Sons.

Heritage, M. (2010). *Formative assessment: Making it happen in the classroom.* Thousand Oaks, CA: Corwin Press.

Hess, E. (1973). *Imprinting: early experience and the developmental psychobiology of attachment.* New York, NY: Van Nostrand Reinhold Company.

Hunter, M. (1982). *Mastery teaching.* El Segundo, CA: TIP Publications.

Hunter, M. (1988). Quote from a live presentation. Raleigh, NC.

Hunter, M. (1994). *Enhancing teaching.* New York, NY: Macmillan College Publishing.

Hunter, M.C., (1994). *Enhancing Teaching.* New York, N.Y. Macmillan College Publishers.

Huttenlocher, P. (2002). *Neural plasticity: The effects of environment on the development of the cerebral cortex.* Cambridge, MA: Harvard University Press.

Hyerle, D. (1996). *Visual tools for transforming information into knowledge.* Thousand Oaks, CA: Corwin Press.

Jenson, E. (1998). *Teaching with the brain in mind.* Alexandria, VA: Association for Supervision and Curriculum Development.

Jenson, E. (2008). *Brain based learning: The new paradigm of teaching.* Thousand Oaks, CA: Corwin Press.

Johnston, J., Markel, G., & Haley-Oliphant, A. (1987). What research says about questioning in the classroom. *Middle School Journal, 18*, 29-33.

Jonassen, D., Tessmer, M., & Hannum, W. (1999). *Task analysis methods for instructional design.* Mahwah, NJ: Erlbaum.

Joyce, B., & Showers, B. (2002). *Student Achievement through Staff Development.* Alexandria, VA: Association for Supervision and Curriculum Development.

Joyce, B., & Showers, B. (2002). *Student achievement through staff development.* Alexandria, VA: Association for Supervision and Curriculum Development.

Karweit, N. (1987). *Implications of time on task research for classroom practice.* Washington, DC: U.S. Department of Education.

Kaufeldt, M. (1999). *Begin with the brain: Orchestrating the learner centered classroom.* Tucson, AZ: Zephyr Press.

Kohn, A. (1993). *Punished by rewards: The trouble with gold stars, incentive plans, A's, praise, and other bribes.* Boston, MA: Houghton Mifflin.

Kohn, A. (1999). *Punished by rewards.* Boston, MA: Houghton Mifflin.

Kohn, A. (2006). *The homework myth.* Cambridge, MA: Da Capo Press.

Landauer, T., & Bjork, R. (1978). Optimal rehearsal patterns in name learning. In M. Gruneberg, P.E. Morris, & R.N. Sykes (Eds.), *Practical Aspects of Memory* (pp.625-632). London: Academic Press.

Larkin, J., Mcdermott, J., Simon, D.P., & Simon, H.A. (1980). Expert and novice performance in solving physics problems. *Science*, (208), 1335-1342.

Larkin, J.H., & Simon, H.A. (1987). Why a diagram is (sometimes) worth ten thousand words. *Cognitive Science, 11*, 65-69.

Latener, R.L & Leon, R. (2005). *The illustrated encyclopedia of confucianism*, Vol. 2: New York, NY: Rosen Publishing Group.

LeDoux, J. (1996). *The emotional brain.* New York, NY: Simon & Shuster.

LeDoux, J. (2003). *The synaptic self: How our brains become who we are.* New York, NY: Penguin.

Leiter, M.P., & Maslach, C. (2006). The impact of interpersonal environment on burnout and organizational commitment. *Journal of Organizational Behavior, 9*(4), 297-308.

MacLean, P. (1978). A mind of three minds: Educating the triune brain. *The 77th Yearbook of the National Society for the Study of Education*, pp. 308-342. Chicago, IL: University of Chicago Press.

Mager, R. (1984). *Goal analysis.* Belmont, CA: Lake Publishing Company.

Maier, R.G. (1994). *Location scouting and management handbook: Television, film, still photography.* Newton, MA: Butterworth-Heinemann.

Martin, L., & Clore, G.L. (2001). *Theories of mood and cognition: A user's guidebook.* Mahwah, NJ: Erlbaum.

Marzano, R.J. (2007). *The art and science of teaching: A comprehensive framework for effective instruction.*

Alexandria, VA: Association for Supervision and Curriculum Development.

Marzano, R.J., Pickering, D.J., & Pollock, J.E. (2001). *Classroom instruction that works: Research based strategies for increasing student achievement.* Alexandria, VA: Association for Supervision and Curriculum Development.

Mastropieri, M.A., & Scruggs, T.E. (1998). Constructing more meaningful relationships in the classroom: Mnemonic research into practice. *Learning Disabilities Research and Practice, 13,* 138-145.

Matchock, R. (2010). Circadian and sleep episode duration influences on cognitive performance following the process of awakening. *International Review of Neurobiology, 93,* 129-151.

McCarthy, B. (1987). *The 4mat system: Teaching to learning styles with right/left mode techniques.* Barrington, IL: EXCEL.

McLeod, S. (2007). *Carl Rogers.* Retrieved from http://www.simplypsychology.org.carl-rogers.html.

Melville, H. (1851). *Moby-Dick.* New York, NY: Harper & Brothers Publishers.

Miller, G.A. (1956). The magical number seven, plus or minus two: Some limits on our capacity for processing information. *Psychological Review, 63,* 81-97.

Milne, L.J., & Milne, M. (1980). *National Audubon Society field guide to insects and spiders North America.* New York, NY: Chanticleer Press.

Nummela, R.M., & Rosengren, T.M. (1986). What's happening in student's brains may redefine teaching. *Educational Leadership, 43,* 49-53.

O'Keefe, J. & Nadal, L. (1978). *The hippocampus as a cognitive map.* Oxford: Clarendon Press.

Oldroyd, J., McElheran, K., & Elkington, D. (2011). The short life of online sales leads. *Harvard Business Review, 3,* 88-89.

Orey, M. (2001). *Information procesing.* In M. Orey (Ed.), *Emerging Perspectives on Learning, Teaching, and Technology.* Retrieved Dec., 2012 from http://projects.coe.uga.edu/epltt/

Page, K. & Dornenburg, A. (2008). *The flavor bible: The essential guide to culinary creativity based on the wisdom of America's most imaginative chefs.* New York, NY: Little, Brown and Company.

Payne, R. (1995). *A framework for understanding poverty.* Highlands, TX: RFT

Pekrun, R. (1992). The impact of emotions on learning and achievement: Towards a theory of cognitive/motivational mediators. *Applied Psychology, 41,* 39-376.

Pilbrow, R. (1991). *Stage Lighting.* New York, NY: Drama Book Publishers.

Pinker, S. (2002). *The blank slate: The modern denial of human nature.* New York, NY: Viking.

Poe, E.A. (1845). The raven. *New York Evening Mirror*, published January 29, 1845.

Popham, J. (2011). *Transformative assessment in action.* Alexandria, VA: Association for Supervision and Curriculum Development.

Raaijmakers, J. and Shifflin, R. (1981). Search of associative memory. *Psychological Review, 88*, 93-104.

Reeves, A. (2011). *Where great teaching begins: Planning for student thinking and learning.* Alexandria, VA: Association for Supervision and Curriculum Development.

Reiner, A. (1990). The triune brain in evolution: Role in paleocerebral functions. *Science, 250*, 303-305.

Richardson, S.S. (1996). *WPI technical theater handbook.* Worchester, MA: Worchester Polytechnic Institute.

Rogers, K. (1978). *The gambler.* Written by Don Schlitz, performed by Kenny Rogers. Released by United Artists in 1978.

Rosenfeld, I. (1988). *The invention of memory.* New York, NY: Basic Books.

Ross-Sheehy, S., Oakes, S.M., & Luck, S.J. (2003). The development of visual short-term memory capacity in infants. *Child Development, 74*, 1807-1822.

Rowe, M.B. (1974). Wait time and rewards as instructional variables, their influence on language logic and fate control: Part II wait-time. *Journal of Research in Science Teaching, 17*, 469-475.

Rutherford, M.A. (1993). *Teaching for meaning.* Unpublished manuscript.

Rutherford, M.A. (1995). *Elements of conscius attention.* Unpublished manuscript.

Rutherford, M.A. (1995). *Creating the learning centered school.* Unpublished manuscript.

Rutherford, M.A. (2001). *Creating the learning centered school.* Unpublished manuscript.

Rutherford, M.A. (2009a). *Developing the artisan teacher.* Unpublished manuscript.

Rutherford, M.A. (2009b). *Design lessons for active engagement.* Unpublished manuscript.

Rutherford, M.A. (2009c). *Fun in the classroom…underrated, I think.* Unpublished manuscript.

Rutherford, M.A. (2010). *How talent friendly is your school?* Unpublished manuscript.

Rutherford, M.A. (2012). *The artisan teacher: A field guide to skillful teaching.* Manuscript in preparation.

Schlechty, P. (2011). *Engaging students: The next level of working on the work.* San Francisco, CA: Jossey Bass.

Schoen, M. (2013). *Your survival instinct is killing you. Retrain your brain to conquer fear, make better decisions, and thrive in the 21st century.* London, U.K.: Hudson Street Press.

Senge, P.M., Kleiner, A., Roberts, C., Ross, R.B., & Smith, B.J. (1994). *The fifth discipline fieldbook.* Garden City, NY: Doubleday.

Shepard, A., Slayton, D., & Barbee, J. (1994). *Moonshot: The inside story of America's race to the moon.* Atlanta, GA: Turner Publishing.

Sime, M. and Boyce, G. (1969). Overt responses, knowledge of results and learning. *Programmed Learning and Educational Technology, 6*(1), 12-19.

Simon, H.A. (1974). How big is a chunk? *Science, 183* (4124), 482-488.

Skinner, B.F. (1937). Two types of conditioned reflex: A response to Konorski and Miller. *The Journal of General Psychology, 16,* 272-279.

Sluckin, W. (1965). *Imprinting and early learning.* Chicago, IL: Aldine Publishing Company.

Smith, S. (1979). Remembering in and out of context. *Journal of Experimental Psychology: Human Learning and Memory, 15,* 460-471.

Sousa, D. (2011). *How the brain learns.* Thousand Oaks, CA: Corwin Press.

Sousa, D. A. (1995). *How the brain learns.* Reston, VA: NASSP.

Sparks, D.& Hirsh, S. (1997). *A new vision for staff development.* Alexandria, VA: Association for Supervision and Curriculum Development.

Springer, S.P., & Deutsch, G. (1993). *Left brain, right brain.* New York, NY: W.H. Freeman.

St. Pierre, B. (1996). *A perfect glass of wine.* Vancouver, BC: Raincoast Books.

Sternberg, S. (1966). High-speed scanning in human memory. *Science, 153,* 652-654.

Sylwester, R. & Choo, J. (1992). What brain research says about paying attention. *Educational Leadership, 50,* 71-75.

Sylwester, R. (1995). A *celebration of neurons: An educator's guide to the human brain.* Alexandria, VA: Association for Supervision and Curriculum Development.

Thomas, H.R., Matthews, C.T., & Ward, J.G. (1986). Learning curve models of construction productivity. *ASCE Journal of Construction Engineering and Management, 112*(2), 245-258.

Tigner, R. (1999). Putting memory research to good use. *College Teaching, 47*, 149-152.

Townsend, J.T., & Fific, M. (2004). Parallel and seriel processing and individual differences in high-speed scanning in human memory. *Perception & Psychophysics, 66*, 953-962.

Tri-Star Pictures. *Jerry Maguire* (1996). Written and Directed by Cameron Crowe.

Tse, D., Langston, R.F., Kakeyama, M., Bethus, I., Spooner, P.A., Wood, E.R., Witter, M.P., & Morris, R.G.M. (2007). Schemas and memory consolidation. *Science, 316*, 76-82. DOI: 10.1126/science.1135935

Tuerk, M.M., & Feigenson, L. (2012). Seven-month old infants chunk items in working memory. *Journal of Experimental Child Psychology, 112*(4), 361-377.

Van Praag, H., Kempermann, G., Gage, F. (2000). Neural consequences of environmental enrichment. *Neuroscience, 1*, 191-198.

Vygotski, L. (1978). *Mind in society*. Cambridge, MA: Harvard University Press.

Vygotski, L. (1986). *Thought and language.* Cambridge, MA: Harvard University Press.

Walberg, H.J. (1988). Synthesis of research of time and learning. *Educational Leadership, 45*(6), 76-85.

Walberg, H.J. (1991a). *Extended learning time.* Washington, DC: U.S. Department of Education.

Weith, M.B. & Zacks, R.T. (2011). Time of day effects on problem solving: when the non-optimal is optimal. *Thinking and Reasoning, 17*, 387-401.

William, D., & Thompson, M. (2007). *Integrating assessment with instruction: What will it take to make it work?* In C.A. Dwyer (Ed.), *The future of assessment: Shaping teaching and learning* (pp. 53-82). Mahwah, NJ: Erlbaum.

Wolfe, P. (2010). *Brain Matters: Translating research into classroom practice.* 2nd ed. Alexandria, VA: Association for Supervision and Curriculum Development.

ACKNOWLEDGEMENTS

This work would not have been possible but for the thousands of teachers who graciously opened their classroom doors for observation of their considerable talents and skills. From these observations, Pam Edwards compiled many of the classroom examples and additional research for inclusion in the online appendices. Suzanne Ward kept Rutherford Learning Group, Inc. on task and on schedule while I took time off to write. Laurette Clark Wolfe provided the excellent illustrations. Many thanks to Morehead State University and especially Dr. David Barnett who continually provided challenging and insightful feedback and support. Special thanks to the three teachers who read much of this work and provided valuable feedback on whether what I was writing was clear and applicable for the teachers and administrators who might read it - my wife, Danette Rutherford, and our two teacher-daughters Allison Ferguson and Emily Johnson.

ELABORATIONS AND EXTRA NOTES
examples, applicatons, implications, connections, questions, adjustments, deeper layers, reactions, times not to ...

ELABORATIONS AND EXTRA NOTES

examples, applicatons, implications, connections, questions, adjustments, deeper layers, reactions, times not to ...

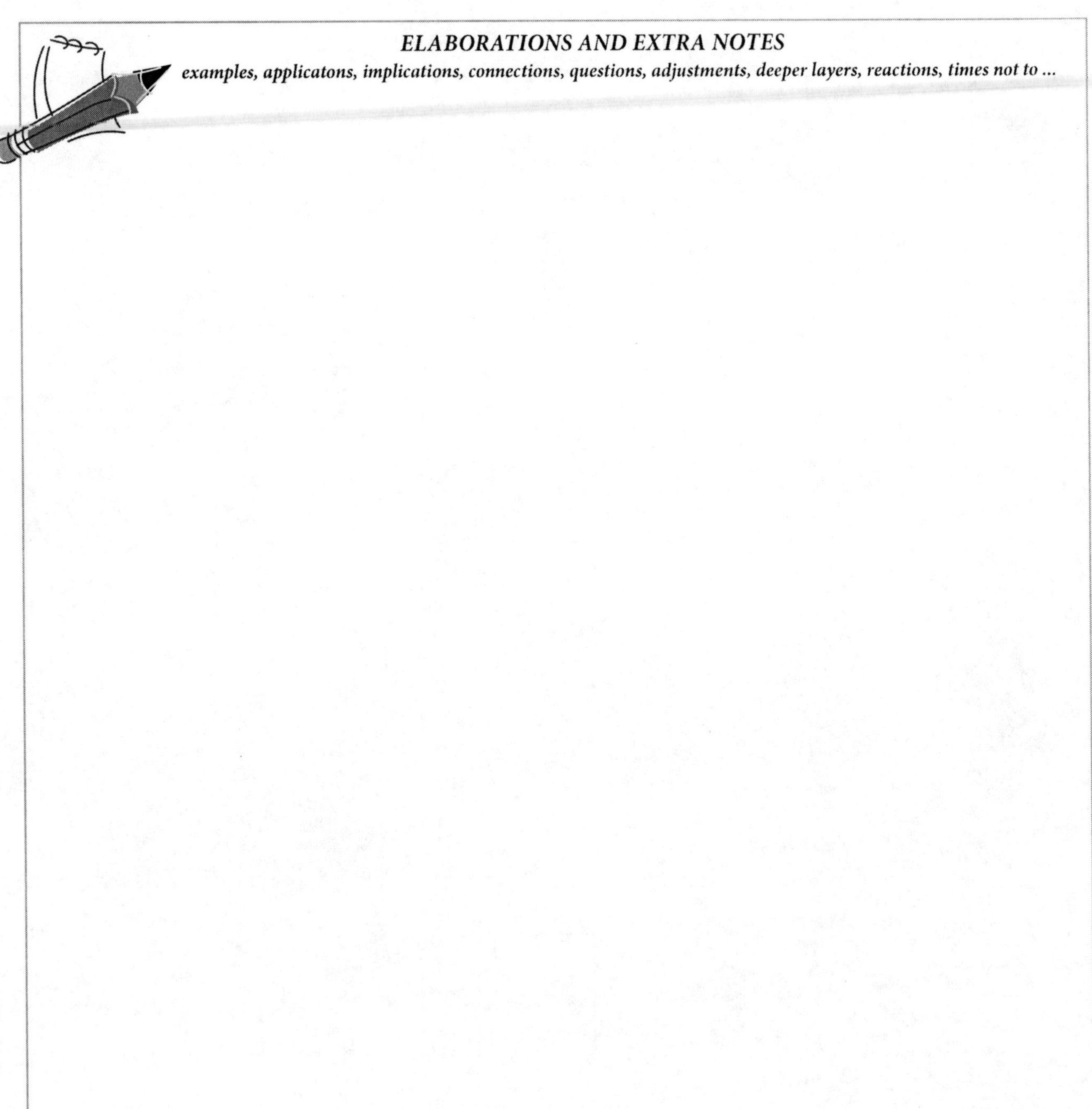
ELABORATIONS AND EXTRA NOTES
examples, applicatons, implications, connections, questions, adjustments, deeper layers, reactions, times not to ...

ABOUT THE AUTHOR

Mike Rutherford, Ed.D. provides high-value training and development experiences for educators and business professionals through his work as a teacher, keynote speaker, author, and consultant. Mike's work focuses on high-performance teaching and learning, leadership development, creating and leading team-based organizations, and results-based organizational improvement. He has created and developed numerous award-winning educational programs for students, teachers, and education leaders including *The Artisan Teacher™*, *Developing the Artisan Teacher™*, *Creating the Learning Centered School™*, *Skillful Observation and Coaching Laboratory™*, *LeaderNext™*, *and Requisites of a Leader™*.

Formerly a high school chemistry teacher, coach, and middle school principal, Mike received a BA in Education from Indiana State University, a MA in Educational Administration from Fayetteville State University, and an Ed.D. in Educational Leadership from Morehead State University.

CPSIA information can be obtained
at www.ICGtesting.com
Printed in the USA
FFOW05n1227070515

9 780991 472406